Irresistible North

Irresistible North

From Venice to Greenland on the Trail of the Zen Brothers

Andrea di Robilant

ALFRED A. KNOPF

NEW YORK

2011

THIS IS A BORZOI BOOK
PUBLISHED BY ALFRED A. KNOPF

Copyright © 2011 by Andrea di Robilant

All rights reserved. Published in the United States by Alfred A.
Knopf, a division of Random House, Inc., New York, and in
Canada by Random House of Canada Limited, Toronto.

www.aaknopf.com

Knopf, Borzoi Books, and the colophon are registered trademarks
of Random House, Inc.

Library of Congress Cataloging-in-Publication Data
Di Robilant, Andrea, [date]
Irresistible North : from Venice to Greenland on the trail of the
Zen brothers / by Andrea di Robilant.—1st ed.
p. cm.
"This Is a Borzoi Book"—T.p. verso.
Includes bibliographical references and index.
ISBN 978-0-307-26985-0
1. North Atlantic Region—Discovery and exploration—
Historiography. 2. Zeno, Nicolò, d. ca. 1395. 3. Zeno,
Antonio, d. ca. 1405. 4. Zeno, Nicolò, 1515–1565.
5. Explorers—Italy—Biography. 6. Faroe Islands—Discovery
and exploration—Historiography. I. Title.
E109.18D57 2011
949.15—dc22   2011000190

Jacket images: *The Battle of Chioggia* (detail) by
Alessandro Grevenbroeck, 1717. Museo Correr,
Fondazione Musei Civici di Venezia; the Zen map, Venice, 1558.
Biblioteca Marciana. Photo Pamela Berry

Jacket design by Evan Gaffney Design

Manufactured in the United States of America
First Edition

For my brothers Filippo and Tristano

Contents

Irresistible North

*The original Zen map, which I found glued to the back of
the 1558 edition of* Dello scoprimento . . .
*It features Frisland, Estland, Islanda, Engronelant,
Estotiland, Drogeo and Icaria.
(See the end of the book for an enlarged map.)*

Prologue

I CAME UPON this curious map in the most unexpected
way. One day I was reading in the Biblioteca Marciana,
in Venice, when an American tourist in shorts and T-shirt
wandered into the hall holding a crumpled piece of paper. I
offered to help as he was having some difficulty making himself understood by the clerk. He said he came from Madison,
a small coastal town in Connecticut; he was on a pilgrimage
to see the family palazzo of two Venetian brothers he
claimed had crossed the Atlantic and reached the coast of
North America at the end of the fourteenth century. He
handed over the note on which he had scribbled their names:
Nicolò and Antonio Zen. They meant nothing to me at the
time and the story sounded rather outlandish, but as the
American was in a hurry to rejoin the group he was with, I
pulled out from the open stacks a book on Venetian palaces,
showed him a picture of a Palazzo Zen near the Frari Church
and sent him on his way.

There are several Zen palaces in Venice: a few days later I
was walking down the Fondamenta Santa Caterina, off the
Campo dei Gesuiti (a brisk twenty-minute walk from the
Frari), when I noticed a soot-covered plaque on the wall of a
crumbling building:

A
Nicolò e Antonio Zen
nel secolo decimoquarto

navigatori sapientemente arditi
dei mari nordici*

So this was the Palazzo Zen the American was looking for! It had none of the majesty of the great palaces that line the Grand Canal. Tufts of weeds tumbled out of the cracks in the marble. Loose electrical wires dangled from on high. Steel beams supported the walls like rusty old crutches. Even by Venetian standards, the building looked terribly worn. Yet the unusual mix of Gothic and Renaissance styles, embellished by Levantine motifs, gave it an air of shabby grandeur.

The next day, I put aside my research and checked the library catalog to see if I could find a reference to the Zen brothers and their mysterious voyages. Out of the Rare Book Collection came a dusty little volume, six inches by four, that seemed to have traveled to my desk straight from a sixteenth-century Venetian bookshop.

The book was printed in 1558 by a certain Francesco Marcolini. It was a travel narrative written in Italian, which was unusual because Latin was still the language of choice in publishing. The title was long-winded but alluring: *Dello scoprimento dell'isole Frislanda, Eslanda, Engrovelanda, Estotilanda & Icaria fatto sotto il Polo Artico da due fratelli Zeni (On the Discovery of the Islands of Frislanda, Eslanda, Engrovelanda, Estotilanda and Icaria made by two Zen brothers under the Arctic Pole).*

The name of the author was not on the cover, but Marcolini, the printer, explained in the introduction that the book was written by "the Magnificent M. Nicolò Zen," a great-great-great-grandson of Antonio Zen, one of the two navigators. This Nicolò Zen, whom I shall henceforth call Nicolò the Younger to avoid confusion with his ancestor,

---

* "To Nicolò and Antonio Zen, wise and courageous navigators to the northern seas in the fourteenth century."

was a well-respected statesman in Renaissance Venice and a minor historian whom I'd come across on several occasions during my studies at the Biblioteca Marciana. The book, he claimed, was based on several damaged letters the brothers had sent home during their travels in the 1380s and 1390s, and which had remained in the family archives ever since.

Glued to the back of the little volume was a *Carta da navegar*—a nautical map. (For an enlargement of this map, see the final page of this book.) It was a wood-engraving with a rich, grainy texture. At first glance it looked like the sketch of an old treasure map, with oddly shaped islands and exotic place names. But I recognized the coastline of Scandinavia. The Shetland Islands were placed a little too close to the Norwegian coast. Iceland was roughly where it should have been, although a cluster of mysterious islets had been sprinkled along its eastern coast. Greenland's outline was traced with startling precision, but then a lumpy Nova Scotia seemed to have lost its bearings and was floating eastward, away from Newfoundland and the coast of New England. Strangest of all was a large, bulky island called Frisland (Frislanda in the text of the book), which the author placed above Scotland.

Even more intriguing than these obvious distortions was the general configuration of the map. It showed the North Atlantic as a semi-enclosed sea, in some ways a mirror image of the Mediterranean, and not as a wide-open expanse of water between two continents. Although the map was in many respects rather advanced by Renaissance standards— especially with regard to Greenland—it seemed to reflect a late-medieval view of the North Atlantic in that it did not take into account the new geographical discoveries that, from 1492 onward, had revealed to Europeans the existence of the American landmass.

Travel narrative was very popular in the sixteenth century and the book sold well. After some initial probing I learned that several editions appeared in Venice in the following years. One of them reached Gerard Mercator, the great cartographer, in the German town of Duisburg; he used the Zens' *Carta da navegar* to complete the first modern map of the world in 1569. An English translation was published in London by Richard Hakluyt, an influential geographer in Elizabethan England. Later I discovered that John Dee, astrologer, mathematician and close advisor to Queen Elizabeth I, seized on the Zen voyages in the 1570s to press the case for a British empire in North America. The Crown even sent Martin Frobisher on a fruitless journey to discover Frislanda and claim it for England.

As cartography became more accurate, the Zen map, like all maps of its period, lost much of its relevance. The book, on the other hand, continued to be read well into the nineteenth century. But in 1835 a Danish admiral, Christian Zahrtmann, stunned the world of geographers and mapmakers by declaring it was nothing but "a tissue of fiction" and that Nicolò the Younger, the author, was a mischievous fablemonger. It took forty years for the Royal Geographical Society to publish a rebuttal of Admiral Zahrtmann's accusations; it was penned by Richard Henry Major, one of its most prestigious members. But the stain of forgery proved indelible. The book suffered several more attacks and by the end of the nineteenth century it had been fairly torn to shreds, a critic pronouncing it "one of the most successful and obnoxious [literary frauds] on record."

The Zen brothers faded into oblivion. There is not a trace of them in contemporary books about travel and discovery. Their names are unknown even to Venetians. And hardly anyone notices the plaque that was unveiled more than 120 years ago on the façade of Palazzo Zen (after R. H. Major's rebuttal of Zahrtmann's thesis).

Yet I found it hard to let go of the story. The more I read about it—about the voyages, the forgery charges, the rehabilitation, the new round of accusations—the more I was puzzled. It seemed to me unreasonable that Nicolò the Younger should have put his reputation at risk for the sake of an elaborate prank. If it was a fake, what could possibly have been the motive behind such a brazen act of fraud? To suggest that his ancestors had reached North America before 1492? But surely Nicolò the Younger would have made that claim explicit at some point. True, the narrative was filled with mistakes and incongruities, some of them rather bewildering. But all maps and travel narratives of the sixteenth century were riddled with befuddling oddities. Could not those very errors be the mark of authenticity rather than deceit? I shared the sympathetic feeling of Alexander von Humboldt, the great German naturalist and geographer of the early nineteenth century, who found the story "to be filled with candor and detailed descriptions" they could not have borrowed from others.

Over and over I found myself wandering to Palazzo Zen for one more look at the fading façade as if those old stones could yield a clue to the mystery. At the library I often set aside my regular work to fish out of the stacks yet another volume about fourteenth-century Venetian merchant navigators. I did not yet realize that this growing obsession would drive me to follow the tracks of the Zen brothers out of the library and away from the streets and canals of Venice, on a voyage to the Great North.

ONE DAY, in the early phase of my obsession, I was about to return the little volume on the Zen voyages to the Rare Book Collection when my attention was caught by the printer's mark. In the pioneering days of publishing, printers in Venice went out of their way to design elaborate, eye-catching marks. It was a way to publicize their books and sharpen their commercial profile. But in this case the printer's mark was notable by any measure: an allegorical composition depicting Calumny, Truth and Time so beauti-

Veritas filia temporis — *Truth is the daughter of Time.*
Francesco Marcolini's printer's mark depicting Time
snatching Truth from the clutches of Calumny.

fully drawn that I fancied it might have been sketched by a
Titian or a Tintoretto or another great master of the Venetian
Renaissance.

It took me a little while to decipher the scene. Calumny,
an evil-looking woman with a thick long tail and a cluster of
writhing snakes in her right hand, was pushing naked Truth
off her cloud. Above them, Time, a muscular and wise deity
with wings, was able to save Truth in extremis by grabbing
her wrist with his right hand while holding an hourglass in
his left.

Prologue

The inscription around the engraving read *Veritas filia temporis*—Truth is the daughter of Time. Surely Marcolini, the printer, could not have chosen an allegory more suited to this tale. It occurred to me that in order to get closer to the truth I would have to begin by learning more about the author of the book I was holding in my hands, as well as the printer and the circumstances that had led to its publication.

CHAPTER ONE

Making a Book

The Author

NICOLÒ THE YOUNGER had reason to be furious. He had taken time off from his government duties to complete the first volume of a series he planned to write on world history, which was to cover the invasion of the Germanic tribes, the fall of Rome and the birth of Venice in the early Middle Ages. The manuscript still needed to be revised but his friend, the printer and publisher Marcolini, had pressed him to have a first look. "He was not pleased with my request," Marcolini later recalled. "But in the end he deemed me worthy of the privilege probably on account of the deep affection I have always harbored for his magnificent House."

In exchange for the opportunity to read the draft, Marcolini promised "not to show it to anyone, let alone publish it." But in the end he could not resist the temptation to beat his competitors, and he secretly obtained permission from the Council of Ten to print *Dell'origine de barbari che distrussero per tutto 'l mondo l'imperio di Roma onde hebbe principio la città di Venetia (On the Origin of the Barbarians who Destroyed Rome's Empire around the World Thereby Giving Birth to the City of Venice).*

Before Nicolò the Younger had time to realize the extent of his imprudence the book was selling briskly in the shops around Saint Mark's Square. "He had been so busy perform-

Nicolò Zen the Younger (1515–1565). The painting is part
of the Kingston Lacy Estate collection, in Dorset (UK).
Formerly cataloged as the "portrait of an unknown
Venetian senator," it was identified in 2008 as Titian's
long-lost portrait of Nicolò Zen the Younger, mentioned
by Giorgio Vasari in Lives of the Artists.

ing his public duties that he had not been able to refine and perfect the manuscript," Marcolini guiltily recounted. "[And so I sent it to press] exactly as I had received it in my hands." The result was a mess: not just typos, errors and shoddy writing but a chaotic layout as well. The last section of the book was printed at the front, making the whole thing incomprehensible.

Nicolò the Younger complained bitterly, telling his friend "how truly distraught he was that his work should see the light in such an imperfect, altered and mangled form." All his life he was a loyal, dutiful and dedicated public servant, devoted to his family and to the Republic. As this episode showed, he also cared deeply about his reputation as a historian of Venice. So I thought it was ironic—tragic from his perspective—that he, of all people, should have gone down in history as a shameless liar, a dangerous forger and, perhaps worst of all, "a trickster whose inventions led countless ships astray."

NICOLÒ THE Younger was born in 1515, when Venice was no longer the mercantile power it had been in the time of his forebears. The gradual shift to a land-based economy in the fifteenth century had led the Republic to expand its territory over most of northern Italy and become embroiled in continental power politics. But after years of war and devastation that had brought Venice to its knees, the new doge, the charismatic Andrea Gritti (ruled 1523–38) was presiding over a period of great renewal—*renovatio* was the Latin buzzword of the age.* The city itself underwent major changes that reflected the new landed wealth. Modern palaces rose on the Grand Canal while the old ones were embellished to follow the new classical fashion. The arts—painting, music, poetry—flourished as never before. And the young book

---

* In the fifteenth century the Venetian Republic expanded its mainland possessions to gain hegemony over the vast and fertile plains of the Po Valley. Pope Julius II felt the papal territories, which bordered in the north with the Republic, were increasingly under threat. In 1509 he formed an alliance with France and Spain, two powerful states which had developed ambitions of their own in northern Italy. The ostensible purpose of the League of Cambrai—after the name of the town where the alliance was signed—was to fight the growing menace of the Ottoman Empire. But the immediate objective was to curb Venetian expansion in northern Italy. The mercenary army in Venice's pay was no match for the league and was crushed at the battle of Agnadello. The Venetian strongholds on the mainland collapsed one after the other. In a matter of weeks, the Republic lost all the territory it had gained in a century of expansion. Many saw the humiliating defeat at Agnadello as God's punishment for the hubris that had infected the Republic, not to mention the loose morals

industry thrived, as dozens of new printers opened for business, transforming Venice into the mecca of publishing.

The Zen family embraced humanism from the start. Pietro, Nicolò the Younger's grandfather and the family patriarch, had a reputation for helping young artists and architects get started in Venice. Caterino, Nicolò's father, was a leading member of the literary establishment. Francesco, Nicolò's uncle, was the architect in the family; after his death, the Zens added the draftsman's compass to the nautical rudder, the laurel and the palm tree that already adorned the family crest.

As a teenager, Nicolò absorbed the intellectual atmosphere at Palazzo Zen. Following the fashion of the times, he was schooled in the sciences as well as the humanities. His special aptitude for mathematics led him to become an accomplished hydraulic engineer. But he also studied Greek and Latin literature, philosophy and poetry; his favorite author, he claimed, was Herodotus, the founder of narrative history.

After completing his studies Nicolò went straight into politics, jump-starting his career in government by arranging to be elected to the post of *savio agli ordini dell'Arsenale* (special commissioner for the Arsenal). His appointment was suspended when it was discovered that he was only twenty-three years old, two short of the minimum legal age for the post. Nicolò appealed to the powerful Council of

---

that had made the city a symbol of greed and depravity. Andrea Gritti, a fiery and courageous young patrician, led the struggle for Venice's redemption. He recaptured Padua and other cities on the mainland. Meanwhile, the League of Cambrai broke apart as the pope and the king of Spain turned against France, their erstwhile ally. Venice seized the moment, siding with the young French king, Francis I. In 1515, the French won a decisive battle at Marignano with the help of the Venetians. As a result, France consolidated its presence in Piedmont while Venice regained most of the provinces lost after Agnadello. The Republic had learned its lesson, though, and it gave up its aggressive expansionism, opting instead for a prudent policy of neutrality.

Ten, invoking a law that allowed candidates to purchase up to five years' experience at the cost of one hundred ducats; he won and was reinstated.

By then, Gritti's enlightened dogeship was coming to an end. Tensions between the western powers and the Ottoman Empire were building in the Mediterranean. Emperor Charles V of Spain, the leader of Christian Europe, cobbled together an alliance to push back the Turks. Venice's policy of peaceful engagement with the Ottoman Empire, which Gritti had upheld with the support of the Zens, dissolved in a warmongering frenzy. "Venetians, especially young ones, [are now] fervently clamoring for war," Nicolò noted with dismay.

The military confrontation—it was hardly a war—turned into a humiliating debacle for the coalition. At Preveza, off the coast of western Greece, the allied commander, the Genoese admiral Andrea Doria, backed out of the fight under orders from Emperor Charles himself, who was secretly negotiating with the Sublime Porte to avoid all-out war. As the junior partner in the alliance, Venice could do little but acquiesce and retreat. But the moment was certainly sobering, for it revealed rather starkly the diminished political status of the Republic.

For young Nicolò, Preveza was a defining experience. Stung by the outcome of the conflict, he wrote a scathing account of the campaign. *History of the War between Venice and the Turks* is not so much a narrative as a vitriolic indictment of those who had pressed for war against the Ottoman Empire and then had behaved so ignominiously in the hour of battle. Nicolò ranted against "the infamy of all Christianity" and called on "the Spanish soldiers who were on the Emperor's ships to bear testimony" to the shameful conduct of the western alliance.

Nicolò's beloved Herodotus would probably have frowned at his overheated prose. In the end, the manuscript was never published and his fierce denunciation was read only, if at all, within the confines of Palazzo Zen. But the copy that survives in the Biblioteca Marciana offers a fascinating glimpse into the mind of this ambitious twenty-five-year-old patrician already fully engaged in the affairs of the Republic.

Although never a merchant himself, Nicolò was very proud of the mercantile origins of his family. To him, trade had been the lifeblood of the Republic since its earliest days and had strengthened it over the centuries. He felt very strongly that by shifting their economy from the sea to the mainland, Venetians had betrayed their roots and corrupted the soul of the Republic. "Now everyone rushes to buy property in order to live on their income," he lamented, "while merchants [are] despised and greatly berated." He blamed this morally impoverished environment for the hubris that had led to war.

Nicolò idealized the early days of the Republic, when Venice was a small democratic community and Venetians lived "in houses of equal size and height, decorated in the same manner." He decried the new fashion of building "palaces and magnificent dwellings," which fostered feelings of inequality—an obvious dig at the new landed aristocracy living in luxury on the Grand Canal. To him, the new palaces were garish symbols of Venice's moral decay. He lambasted the fashionable young architects who indulged in the so-called ornamental style; ever the moralist, he railed against "the indolent and the pleasure-seeking" who mixed with singers and actors and courtesans.

Nicolò's militant brand of nostalgia was no doubt sharpened by the fire of youth. But old republican values had always thrived at Palazzo Zen, and Nicolò had absorbed them from his grandfather, the venerable Pietro, and from his father, Caterino. Palazzo Zen was a household where *renovatio* did not mean renewal for renewal's sake but rather through the rediscovery of the virtues and traditions of the early Republic.

At twenty, Nicolò had married Elisabetta Contarini, a member of one of the oldest Venetian families. She bore him a son, Caterino, ensuring the line would continue into the next generation. By the early 1540s, Nicolò was already looked upon as the leading representative of the Zen family, "whose great worth and wisdom," wrote a contemporary chronicler, "everyone in Venice admires."

His government career progressed rapidly. He was sent on his first mission abroad, to the court of Charles V in Madrid, to patch up relations with Spain after the fiasco of the war against Turkey. He made a lasting impression on the emperor, and if he still felt the urge to inveigh against "all Christianity," as he had in the wake of defeat, he evidently bit his tongue.

Back in Venice, Nicolò joined the Collegio della Milizia da Mar, a commission established to oversee the reorganization of the Arsenal and the rebuilding of the Venetian fleet. In his view, the Arsenal was to be much more than just a great shipyard: he saw it as the hinge that would join Venice's sea and land power. He set himself to the task "with loving diligence and practical wisdom," in the words of one observer, and was often to be found in one of the yards at the Arsenal taking notes among the *arsenalotti,* measuring planks, weighing materials, testing pulleys to find new ways of "lifting huge weights with as little effort as possible." It is doubtful the production target of 130 warships—roughly the size of the Ottoman fleet and slightly smaller than the Spanish Armada—was reached during his tenure or indeed afterward. But his thoughtful policies were credited with transforming the Arsenal into a leaner and more efficient ship-building machine.

Next, he turned his "good judgment" to improving the web of waterways in the lagoon. Over the centuries, the silt deposits brought in by the Piave and its tributaries had altered the sand and mud formations around the city. The haphazard dredging of new canals had further changed the seascape, dangerously affecting water levels. Nicolò was elected several times *savio di terraferma* and *savio alle acque*—land commissioner and water commissioner—key posts that enabled him to dominate the public debate on this issue during the 1540s and 1550s. He drew plans for reclaiming vast tracts of marshland and managed to renovate the lagoon's complex hydraulic system.

Nicolò brought a humanistic approach to his scientific and managerial tasks. He was interested in a general reorganization of the city and its territory and he drew on his classical education to give depth and range to his technical solutions. Even though he was known primarily as an engineer, his Pliny and his Vitruvius were never out of reach.

Yet for all his dedication to Venice's renewal, the pull of the past was always strong. All his life Nicolò sought ways to celebrate the fabled story of the Republic—making sure his family's important role in it was remembered as well. His book on the origins of Venice was meant above all as a tribute to the city he loved. That the publication turned out to be a complete fiasco would have been especially painful and humiliating for him.

Marcolini had put his friendship with Nicolò at risk for the sake of a book. But he had taken a precaution by dedicating the volume to the patriarch of Aquileia, Daniele Barbaro, who served as archbishop of Venice. Barbaro was a well-known humanist and a distinguished former diplomat. He was also Nicolò's closest friend. Marcolini hoped Barbaro would talk to his "soul mate" and "appease his rage in the face of my disobedience, much like Daniel appeased the ferocious lion." The ploy worked, and Nicolò eventually forgave his publisher. The following year Marcolini printed a new edition of the book, revised and corrected, this time with the author's approval. And if Nicolò is remembered at all as a historian, it is on the strength of that one volume on Venetian history.

Marcolini's Shop

IN THE BIBLIOTECA MARCIANA I found a woodprint of Marcolini carved when he was in his late thirties or early for-

*Francesco Marcolini's portrait
adorned the frontispiece of the 1540
edition of* Le Sorti.

ties. The portrait itself is very fine and conveys Marcolini's
energy and quick intelligence. He was a handsome man, with
a wide forehead, a large, well-proportioned nose and an
inquisitive expression. His hair was thick and curly, and like
many of his contemporaries, he wore a long beard. The portrait has a Titian-like feel to it and although there is no certainty about the authorship, some scholars attribute it to the
great Venetian master.

Marcolini, I learned, was originally from Forlì, a small
city in Romagna that had fallen on bad times during the rule
of Caterina Sforza. For a talented young man interested in
the book business, the obvious place to go was Venice, where
relative intellectual freedom provided a more permissive
atmosphere. He arrived around 1525, in the heyday of Doge
Gritti's *renovatio.* Aldus Manutius, the father of modern
publishing, had died, but the industry was still very vibrant.
There were no less than 150 printers operating in Venice
at the time, many of them doubling as publishers. More

books were being printed there than in any other European city.

Marcolini entered the fray with considerable brio, quickly establishing himself as a quality printer and publisher in the expanding market of music books and scores. Soon he opened his own print shop, next to the friars of the Order of the Cruciferi, whose oratory abutted Palazzo Zen. Pietro Zen, Nicolò's grandfather, took the young printer under his wing; years later Marcolini readily acknowledged he was "a creature of the great Pietro."

He invested his earnings in a new printing press and a complete set of Garamond type, purchased wood blocks to make engravings and hired Johannes Britus, a talented German engraver, to embellish his books. Marcolini himself was an accomplished artist, a draftsman and a goldsmith, and all his skills found expression in his print shop, where he worked late into the night, his hands covered in ink and sticky with glue, designing letter blocks for his chapter headings or preparing a collection of decorative friezes. He was not always a careful editor and his copy was often filled with mistakes he later had to correct (I noticed the list of errata in each of his books was usually very long), but he made a point of publishing beautifully designed and finely executed volumes, fretting endlessly about the title, the layout, the type. He promoted his books with enticing prefaces and blurbs.

Marcolini's big break came in the early 1530s, when he first published Pietro Aretino, a literary celebrity who had been run out of Rome by Pope Clement VII after the publication of his popular *Sonnetti Lussuriosi* (*Lewd Sonnets*). Aretino arrived in Venice preceded by his fame. He was a talented satirist who delighted his readers with his impudence and irreverence toward the rich and powerful—although, when necessary, he knew how to ingratiate himself with them as well. His many patrons, among them the king of France, Francis I, lavished money and gifts on him in part because they feared his vitriolic pen. A larger-than-life character, he lived in great style, enjoyed a rich table and, as we shall see, was not above seducing the wives of his friends. Marcolini met Aretino shortly after the writer had settled in Venice and quickly came under his spell. It was Aretino who persuaded him to start his own print shop. As a mark of his friendship, and of his confidence in his publishing talent, he offered him the manuscript of *La Cortigiana* (*The Courtesan*), an uproarious comedy about life among the lower classes in papal Rome. Marcolini published it in 1534 and it became a runaway best seller. During the next decade, he published a dozen other books by Aretino, his star author.

While the Zens provided Marcolini with useful contacts in the upper reaches of the ruling oligarchy, Aretino introduced him to his artistic circle, which included Titian, Tintoretto, Sebastiano del Piombo and Jacopo Sansovino. This talented band of artists, writers and architects would gather in Marcolini's print shop after a day's work for a mug of wine and some boisterous conversation, which often continued at the young publisher's home, where his beautiful wife Isabella gave everyone dinner.

It was a joyful period for Marcolini. His reputation as a quality printer and publisher grew and he made good money in the process. His own creativity found an easy and gratifying outlet in the production of his beautiful editions. He also became an accomplished goldsmith and developed a serious interest in architecture, even designing a bridge that was built over a canal on the island of Murano. "Our friend Francesco's superb structure has finally given a soul to the body of Murano," Aretino wrote to Sansovino, Venice's chief public architect. In 1540 Marcolini authored his only book, *Le Sorti intitolate giardino dei pensieri* (*The Cards of Fate in the Garden of the Mind*), a society game published as a book of cards. Learned and playful, it was illustrated with splendid drawings—the hallmark of the Marcolini publishing house. No less a critic than Giorgio Vasari, the great Renaissance art historian, weighed in to praise *Le Sorti*'s "beautiful imagery."

Then something went terribly wrong in Marcolini's

happy world. From the half statements and innuendos that surface in letters of the period, it appears that his beloved wife, Isabella, succumbed to Aretino's insistent sexual demands. What we know for sure is that Marcolini shut down his print shop, left Venice in a hurry with his wife and sailed to Cyprus (then under Venetian rule), where he took on a clerkship in the governor's office. Aretino wrote several letters to Marcolini begging him to come back. But he did not return to Venice until four years later, in 1549. By then Isabella was dead—she must have died in Cyprus or on the way home.

Marcolini opened for business again but never really made up with Aretino and did not publish any new work of his. Anton Francesco Doni, a writer of popular romances, became his new best-selling author. Doni's fanciful love stories could not have been more different from Aretino's biting satires and lewd poems. But they sold well, each edition running into several thousand copies. Marcolini continued to have one of the more interesting lists in town—a mixture of novels, biographies and narrative history—but it was certainly not as spicy and irreverent as it had been during his early years as a publisher (his backlist remained impressive, with works by Dante, Boccaccio, Petrarch, Ariosto, as well as classics by Aristotle, Polybius, Ovid, Cicero and his beloved Vitruvius).

After his return from Cyprus, Marcolini renewed his ties with the Zens. Nicolò the Younger had been a teenager when he had last seen him; now he was the head of the family and a man of influence in Venice. Marcolini cultivated his friendship, even boasting to his readers that he had "not a little familiarity with this very noble and kind-hearted gentleman." After the row over the unauthorized publication of Nicolò's volume on the history of Venice, the two men, as we have seen, renewed their close ties. And it was to Marcolini that Nicolò eventually turned two years later when he decided to publish an account of his forebears' travels in the North Atlantic.

Ramusio's World

THERE WAS PROBABLY no better place than Venice to gain a sense of how the view of the world was changing in the mid-sixteenth century. True, the Republic was not a player in the Age of Discovery. Portugal, Spain, France and England were the new great naval powers driving world exploration. Still, if Venice no longer had the ambition and the resources to finance expensive expeditions to distant lands, it was nevertheless the major clearinghouse for the valuable information flowing back to Europe: information circulated more freely than in any other European capital. An endless stream of travel narratives, captain's diaries, ship's logs, maps and portolan charts found their way to Venice, which in turn had the printing presses, the publishers, the editors, the bookbinders, the illustrators, the mapmakers to process and disseminate the new literature of exploration.

The most ambitious publishing project in the 1550s was Giovanni Battista Ramusio's monumental *Delle navigationi et viaggi* (*On Journeys and Navigations*). Ramusio was one of Venice's highest-ranking and most respected civil servants. In the course of his long career in government he had collected the reports of the major European explorers, translated them into Italian and edited them carefully (while still a student, he had worked as an apprentice in Manutius's print shop, reading and selecting manuscripts and preparing them for publication).

Poring over his travel narratives, Ramusio had reached the conclusion that the old Ptolemaic world was "quite inaccurate with respect to the knowledge we have today." He decided to use the vast material in his possession to produce a written geography of the world that cartographers could use as a source for a new mapping of the globe. "I think it would be good and not a little useful," he explained, "to assemble the narratives of our time written by those who

Giovanni Battista Ramusio
"stole time from Time itself" to complete Delle
navigationi et viaggi, *his three-volume collection of*
travel narratives. This medal was printed in the
Museum Mazzucchellianum, *an eighteenth-*
century museum catalog.

have actually been in those regions and have described them
in detail."

As Ramusio saw it, the world beyond Europe was
roughly divided into three parts: Africa, India and Brazil to
the south; Asia and Scandinavia to the north and east; the
New World to the west. Accordingly, he planned one volume for each geographical area, in that order. The first one
came out in 1550. It was a sensation, in part because it
included a considerable scoop: Leo Africanus's report on his
extraordinary journey across Africa.

Al Hasan ben Mohammad al Wazzan az Zayati, later
known as Leo Africanus, came from a well-to-do Arab family living in Spain. After the fall of Granada in 1492, the family moved to Fez, in Morocco, where young Hasan was

educated. He later traveled across Africa on commercial and diplomatic missions, but on a voyage home he was captured by pirates and sold as a slave. His new owner was so impressed by his learning that he presented him as a gift to Pope Leo X. The pontiff freed him in exchange for his conversion to Christianity and christened him Giovanni Leone. The former slave became a fixture in Roman humanistic circles. He wrote a Latin version of *Description of Africa,* the fascinating chronicle of his voyages, but the pope kept the manuscript under lock. So it was quite a coup for Ramusio to get his hands on it, thanks to his secret contacts in Rome.

CONSUMED BY the demands of his regular job as an influential secretary at the Senate, Ramusio pressed on with the preparation of the next two volumes of his trilogy "by stealing time from Time," as his printer, Tommaso Giunti, put it.

Unlike Ramusio, Nicolò the Younger had been slow to understand the extraordinary changes taking place in the world as a result of the geographical discoveries of the first half of the century — including the rapid decline of Venice as a great naval power. His own vision of the world remained centered around the Mediterranean; he had little patience with the hoopla surrounding the Spanish conquests in the New World. "The Spaniards," he wrote as late as 1540, "tell us there are many countries, islands and provinces there." But he had been to Spain and knew better. "They are bombastic by nature. They brag and are untruthful." Imprudently, he added, "Of one thing I am sure: they have found much less than what they claim."

However, by the time the first volume of Ramusio's trilogy came out, Nicolò was belatedly catching on. He now acknowledged the importance of the discovery of "so many territories where we least expected to find them." Marveling at the success of Ramusio's first volume, he thought it would be a good idea to offer an edited version of "the documents I have been able to salvage" on the voyages of his forebears.

There was not much left: five badly damaged letters and a barely legible chart. According to Nicolò, he was largely responsible for the awful condition of those precious family heirlooms: "When I was a child I took those papers in my hands, and not knowing what they were, I tore and damaged them, as a child will do. To this day the very thought of what I did causes me the greatest sorrow." He must have received quite a scolding if, so many decades later, he was still grieving for the wreckage he had caused. And given what I knew of Nicolò—his sense of duty, his diligence, an earnestness that verged on naïveté—it is hard for me to escape the feeling that the publication of the Zen voyages was, at least in part, an act of belated atonement.

Nicolò set about rearranging, editing and weaving the content of what remained of the five surviving letters into a unified narrative, padding generously and adding new information along the way. He then drew a map of the region where the travels took place, based "on an old and rotten chart we still had in our house," but no doubt consulting other cartographic sources available to him. "I think it's come out rather well," he noted, pleased with himself. "It will certainly enlighten interested readers who might otherwise have trouble understanding the narrative." To be sure, the Zen map had its share of incongruities. But Nicolò had reason to be satisfied: by contemporary standards it appeared to be a great step forward in the geographical knowledge of the North Atlantic.

RAMUSIO'S MUCH-ANTICIPATED second volume of the *Navigationi et viaggi* was mostly devoted to Asia. It was built around Marco Polo's travels but it included more recent reports on Persia, Tartary, Russia and the Black Sea by Venetian ambassadors. Scandinavia was also part of the volume because it was considered an extension of the Asian continent. Thus Nicolò's labor of love seemed a perfect fit: after all, Frislanda, Estlanda, Islanda, Engroneland and

Estotiland* were seen as an extension of the Scandinavian world. Ramusio, who knew Nicolò well through their work in the Senate, was familiar with the voyages of the Zen brothers. Although there is no evidence that he ever planned to include them in the second volume of his collection, I imagine he was certainly open to the idea and discussed the matter with his closest friends and advisors.†

However, the publication of that second volume was plagued by delays. Ramusio, who did not want to keep his readers waiting, decided to go ahead with the third volume, on the New World, which included firsthand accounts of Columbus's voyages and narratives by Peter Martyr, Oviedo de Guzmán, Hernán Cortés, Cabeza de Vaca, Francisco Coronado, Giovanni da Verrazano and Jacques Cartier. Volume three came out successfully in 1556.

One possible cause for the long delay in the publication of the second volume—but this is mere conjecture on my part—were the secret negotiations Ramusio was carrying forward at the time. In the early 1550s, shortly after the publication of the first volume of *Navigationi et viaggi,* the Republic contacted Sebastian Cabot and discreetly put forward the idea that he lead a Venetian exploratory mission to find a northwest passage to Cathay under the Arctic Pole. Sebastian, a Venetian citizen then living in England, was the obvious candidate for the job. Son of John Cabot, who had reached North America in 1497, he was a great navigator and explorer in his own right. Initial talks with the Venetian ambassador in London were encouraging and the parties decided they should be continued in Venice. Ramusio was

---

* In earlier centuries, spelling was nonstandardized, and sources offer several variants for the place-names in the Zen story. To avoid confusion, I have selected one spelling for each to use throughout this book, except when quoting directly from a text or map: Frislanda, Engroneland, Islanda, Estotiland, and Drogio.

† In the early 1550s these would have been his publisher, Tommaso Giunti, and his closest friend, the humanist Girolamo Fracastoro, who first brought the Zen voyages to his attention.

entrusted with this delicate dossier, possibly on account of his geographical knowledge. The immediate task was to find a pretext to bring Sebastian to Venice without raising suspicions in London. It was decided that the Seigneury would summon him to settle certain matters related to family properties.

In any discussion about the search for a northwest passage, Ramusio and indeed Sebastian himself are bound to have brought up the voyage of the Zen brothers. And it is unlikely Ramusio would have agreed to make the Zen narrative and the map public while the Republic was secretly trying to set up a mission to that region. By 1556, however, talks with Sebastian had broken down, possibly because the English ambassador in Venice, having been informed of the talks by his spies at the Doge's Palace, had managed to scuttle them. It does not appear Sebastian came to Venice. Instead, he turned his attention to the Arctic Sea north of Russia and helped to organize several unsuccessful expeditions to find a northeast passage to China.

As it turned out, the fruitless talks with Sebastian were to be Venice's last, half-hearted attempt to play a role in the Age of Discovery.

THE FOLLOWING summer, Ramusio retreated to the peace and quiet of his villa near Padua to finish editing the intractable second volume. But he developed a case of petechia and purplish spots soon appeared all over his body. He weakened very quickly—he may have contracted typhoid fever as well—and on July 10 he died, leaving the work unfinished.

Tommaso Giunti, the printer, was devastated by the death of his close friend and associate. He assured his readers that the ill-starred second volume would be available by the end of the year, but on November 4, 1557, a devastating fire broke out among the presses and the print shop was reduced to a pile of ashes. Giunti was inconsolable. "The loss has been very substantial," he lamented. "Several of the texts which Ramusio had prepared and were ready to go to press went up in flames together with a number of maps."

Was the story of the Zen voyages among those destroyed by the fire? In the light of the controversy that has surrounded the Zen map for so long, the question takes on more than a mere bibliographical interest. It would have been useful to know whether Ramusio, a very diligent and widely respected editor, had actually gone through the material himself and put his stamp of approval on it before dying. In the absence of any evidence one can only guess what his opinion might have been.

As a rule, Ramusio preferred to publish eyewitness accounts drawn from original manuscripts. Admittedly, Nicolò had used fragments of five badly damaged letters and a chart to stitch together a narrative. That alone would probably not have disqualified the story: Ramusio readily acknowledged that many manuscripts came to him "damaged and filled with mistakes," and this did not prevent him from publishing them, usually after very intense editing sessions. "I hesitate a long time before publishing the documents I receive," he explained, "because I cannot swear on the quality of the material. But after hesitating, I usually let myself be swayed by my desire to leave for future generations information that might turn out to be useful to them."

Still, my feeling is that Ramusio had decided to leave the Zen story out of the second volume. Not so much because he didn't find it convincing—his editorial policy, we have just seen, was "when in doubt, print"—but because it was a heavily edited text prepared by someone other than himself. By his own admission, Ramusio was a hands-on editor, a perfectionist who worked on his texts obsessively during his "many sleepless nights." He would have resisted the inclusion in his series of a story "packaged" by another editor— even an eminent Venetian like Nicolò.

The truth is that by the early summer of 1557, only days before Ramusio's death and weeks before the fire at the

Giunti press, Nicolò was already making plans to publish the story elsewhere. Who did he call on? Marcolini, of course, who immediately petitioned the Council of Ten for permission to print. The Riformatori dello Studio di Padova—the commission in charge of overseeing printing rights—sent the manuscript to two of their habitual readers: Nicolò Robusto Cipriota, a Carmelitan monk, and Alfonso de Ulloa, a freelance translator of Spanish texts. Both readers thought the book was "worthy to be printed as there is nothing against religion, good morals or the State."*

Marcolini must have been thrilled by this unexpected turn of events. I checked his list for 1558 and it was rather dull: a life of the doges, a new edition of Nicolò Zen's book on the origins of Venice and a couple of classics—Ovid's *Metamorphoses* and Cicero's *Epistles*. The Zen voyages were just what he needed to jazz things up a little. He went straight to work and by the end of the year produced what turned out to be one of the season's hits. The book was

---

* A reader's job was not without peril in those days. Three years later Cipriota was forbidden to preach because he had approved the publication of *I Dialoghi Segreti*, a book by Pompeo della Barba di Pescia that was later deemed irreverent, confiscated and burned. A far more tragic destiny awaited Ulloa, a Spaniard who had come to Venice as a young man in 1547 and had found employment as secretary to the Spanish ambassador, Don Juan Hurtado de Mendoza. The embassy became a hotbed of intrigue and propaganda. Mendoza was recalled to Madrid and the new ambassador, Don Francisco de Vargas, got rid of Ulloa, who found employment as a Spanish translator with Giolito, a well-known Venetian publisher. To complement his income, Ulloa took on a part-time job as a reader for the Riformatori dello Studio di Padova. The job would cost him his life. In 1568 the Council of Ten ordered his arrest because five years earlier he had approved for publication a book in Hebrew that the Inquisition later decided should not have been published. The accusation was couched in very nebulous terms and appears to have been a mere pretext (by the late 1560s the government had become more intolerant and repressive in the face of new international tensions, especially between Venice and Spain). The hapless Ulloa was sentenced to death. He managed to smuggle out of prison a letter to King Philip II in which he pleaded his innocence and begged him to intercede on his behalf. The letter did not reach Philip in time: Ulloa died of fevers in his prison cell.

printed in an elegant italic type; it had a clean layout and lovely decorative motifs. Marcolini was an experienced copywriter and he assured his readers they would discover "wondrous things about wars and cultures, about the way people live and the clothes they wear, about landscapes and animals and many varieties of fish under the Arctic Pole, where the cold is very great and there is much ice and snow."*

* The volume actually contained two narratives. The first one described the embassy of Caterino Zeno to the court of Uzun Hasan, king of Persia, in the 1470s (*On the Commentaries to the Journey in Persia of M. Caterino Zeno and the Wars Undertaken in the Persian Empire from the Time of Uzun Hasan*). This book, too, was dedicated to Daniele Barbaro, who had been Venetian ambassador to England before becoming the patriarch of Aquilea, and was among the most informed Venetians about the history and geography of the North Sea.

CHAPTER TWO

Messer Nicolò

*After the war against the Genoese that so engaged our elders,
Messer Nicolò, a man of noble spirit, developed a great desire
to see the world & travel & learn the customs and languages
of men, so that he might better serve his fatherland if the
occasion should arise, as well as earn much honor & fame.
And so, having built and equipped a ship with his own riches,
which were very considerable, he left our seas and after
passing the Strait of Gibraltar sailed for several days in the
Ocean to see England & Flanders.*

—Nicolò the Younger, *Dello scoprimento*

O N A LATE SPRING MORNING at high tide, a well-
stocked Venetian round-bodied ship sailed out of
St. Mark's Basin, past the Lido and into the green-
grcy Adriatic Sea. On the poop deck the captain and owner,
Messer Nicolò, charted a southern course on his way to the
Sea of Flanders as the gulls soared and swooped over the
receding lagoon.

The opening scene of this Venetian saga comes readily to
mind. But what sort of a man was Messer Nicolò that he
should be setting out on such a hazardous journey instead of
retiring to enjoy his family and his wealth after four long
years of war against the Genoese (1378–81)? Nicolò the
Younger does not tell us much at all about his forefather
beyond the fact that his riches "were very considerable" and

that he wished "to see the world [and] earn much honor and fame."

I looked for references to Messer Nicolò in the fourteenth-century public record in the State Archives of Venice, at the Frari, and found that he had several namesakes, all more or less distant relatives, all living in Venice at the time. Threading together an outline of his life seemed problematic. How could I be sure I was following the tracks of the right Nicolò Zen? Fortunately, the state clerks of the Republic had to deal with the same confusion of names back in the 1300s. They resolved the problem by adding Nicolò's colorful patronymic—Draconis, son of Dragon—in all official documents. I began to put together little scraps of information—appointments, sales, deeds, wills, birth and death notices—that referred exclusively to Nicolò Zen, son of Dragon, and the story of his adventurous life gradually took shape.

Messer Nicolò must have been in his mid-fifties when he left for the Sea of Flanders. He had built his fortune trading spices in the Levant and was indeed known in the family as *il ricco,* "the rich one." I gained the impression, from the few archival documents available, that he was a man of considerable courage and ingenuity, an expert navigator, a savvy businessman, and a provident husband and father. Commerce in the fourteenth century was not always a peaceful activity; a good Venetian merchant needed to be as much a soldier as a businessman, and Messer Nicolò had his share of rough encounters at sea. Clearly the Republic valued his ability and his experience and turned to him for help in times of both war and peace. Yet I had the feeling he answered the call of duty only if it did not interfere with his own plans and was inclined by temperament to strike out on his own, to bend the rules, to test the patience of the Republic in the pursuit of his goals.

The Zens were among the oldest families in Venice. They settled in the lagoon in early medieval times and played an important role in the affairs of the Republic as it grew and spread its influence in the Adriatic and then in the Mediterranean. Nicolò's most famous ancestor, Raniero Zen, was a key figure behind the development of Venice's merchant marine and went on to become one of the great doges of the thirteenth century.

In Messer Nicolò's time, the family was still among the most powerful in Venice. His father, Pietro Zen, was a charismatic admiral and military commander. He was known as the Dragon because of the fiery beast painted on his shield, which he had wrested from a Genoese captain in hand-to-hand combat. Pietro and his first wife, Agnese Dandolo, had three children: Carlo, Nicolò and Antonio. Agnese died in 1334. The three boys were brought up by Pietro's second wife, Andreola Contarini. The family lived in the neighborhood of Santi Apostoli, just north of the Rialto, the bustling financial and commercial center.

Pietro the Dragon suffered an awful death. In 1343 he led an allied force of Venetian, Genoese, papal and French ships against the Turks, who had taken Smyrna and were threatening trade in the Aegean Sea. He managed to recapture Smyrna, forcing the Turks to retreat. But they did not go far. When the Christian soldiers gathered outside the city to attend a Mass of thanksgiving, the Turks fell on them and hacked them to pieces. According to one source, Pietro was not killed during Mass but while torching enemy ships in the Bay of Smyrna. Whatever the circumstances, his head was cut off and hoisted on a pike and paraded on the grounds of the massacre.

Pietro's death threw the family into a period of hardship and penury. Messer Nicolò, still a teenager, probably joined a merchant galley as a trainee—a common first step for a young nobleman destined for a career at sea. Carlo, his restless brother, was granted a canonry in Patras by Pope Clement VI and sent to study theology at the University of Padua. But he was not made for religious studies and spent his time drinking and gambling in the city's seedier taverns. Antonio, the youngest, was no more than a boy and presumably still living with his stepmother, Andreola.

The 1340s were a bleak decade. The on-again, off-again war with the Genoese crippled trade and seriously hurt the Republic's finances. But much worse was to come. In 1348 the bubonic plague swept through Europe and in little over a year killed 60,000 Venetians—half the population. An eerie silence fell over the city as boats filled with swollen corpses drifted along the canals. But by the spring of 1350 Venetians and Genoese were already at each other again. This time war broke out over access to the rich markets in the Black Sea. Messer Nicolò, by then in his twenties, distinguished himself in combat and after peace was signed with Genoa, in 1355, he obtained an important military command in Romagna, on the Adriatic coast.

Messer Nicolò's talent for commerce, stifled by pestilence and war, was finally able to flourish sometime in the early 1360s, when he was already in his thirties. Venice's trade routes to Egypt, Syria, Cyprus and Romania (via the Black Sea) formed a thriving web across the eastern Mediterranean. Messer Nicolò opened for business on the Rialto, starting out as an agent and intermediary for wealthy merchants. After the death of his stepmother, Andreola, he received financial backing from her two surviving sisters, Orsa and Elisabetta, and made successful investments in galleys trading in the Levant.

At about the same time he married Fantina Muazzo, a young noblewoman from the parish of San Giovanni Grisostomo. They bought a house on Campo S. Fantin and had four children: Antonio, Giovanni, Tommaso and Chiara. By the end of the 1360s, Messer Nicolò had made enough money that he could lease a state-owned galley headed for the port of Tana, in the Sea of Azov, for the handsome sum of thirty golden ducats. During the following years, he led three more commercial convoys to the Black Sea.

It was probably on account of his experience in the eastern Mediterranean that Messer Nicolò was appointed minister of the marine for the Levant in 1378, just months before war with the Genoese broke out anew over access to the Black Sea. The war was to last four years and bring Venice to near collapse. When victory would finally be snatched from the Genoese, Carlo Zen, Messer Nicolò's brother, would be the hero of the day. But Messer Nicolò too was to play an important role in that historic conflict.

The Venetians scored a few initial victories, but in the fall of 1378, Admiral Vettor Pisani's fleet of twenty-four galleys was destroyed by the Genoese in a surprise attack at Pula, a port that faced Venice directly across the northern Adriatic. Pisani made his way back home with no more than five or six badly damaged galleys and was promptly thrown into prison for having failed the Republic so ignominiously. Seizing the favorable turn, the Genoese quickly closed in on Venice. They occupied Chioggia, the port city at the south end of the Venetian lagoon, and were poised to launch the final offensive.

Venice, now desperate, could do little but place its faith in Carlo Zen, who, it turned out, had played no small part in the outbreak of the war. After a failed student life in Padua and a short-lived marriage, Carlo had spent seven years trading and scheming in Constantinople. His close ties to the weak Byzantine emperor John V Palaeologus had eventually paved the way for Venice's military occupation of Tenedos, a fortified island strategically located at the entrance of the Dardanelles. The Genoese had seen the occupation of the island as an intolerable provocation and a good-enough reason to break the twenty-three-year-long truce with their archenemy.

In the early stages of the war the Venetian Senate had sent Carlo out with a small force of no more than six galleys to inflict damage on the Genoese wherever he could find them in the Mediterranean. While the Genoese laid siege to Venice,

Carlo had gone about his business, sinking a small enemy fleet off the coast of Sicily, chasing more galleys all the way up to the Ligurian Sea and making his way to the Aegean.

Messer Nicolò was instructed to slink out of Venice, evade the lurking Genoese ships in the Adriatic and lead a six-galley flotilla to the eastern Mediterranean. He was to join forces with his brother at Tenedos and come back to rescue the Republic with as powerful a fleet as they could assemble. He left in the spring of 1379, nearly a year into the war.

Daniele di Chinazzo, a well-known chronicler of the war, was aboard one of Messer Nicolò's ships and he transcribed the log of their journey. His brief entries were usually fairly mundane but here and there were vivid details that helped me imagine what fourteenth-century navigation was often like. Messer Nicolò's flotilla left on June 10 and sailed down the Adriatic coast, stopping for supplies in Rimini and Ortona, "where we accosted a ship laden with cheeses, which we duly purchased." On June 23 they reached the port of Methoni, a fortified Venetian citadel on the western coast of the Peloponnese; it was known, with nearby Koroni, as "the two eyes of the Republic." The small fleet then rounded Cape Matapan and headed north to the Aegean. At the end of June, it encountered three Catalan ships at Altoluogo (today's Ayasoluk, north of Smyrna). "We raided the ships but returned most of the goods." The Venetians showed no such compunction days later when they ran into a Turkish ship; this time "the men were chopped to pieces and the vessel was sunk." After surviving "a bombardment of heavy rocks" at Chios, they reached the island of Tenedos on July 10.

Carlo Zen, however, was not there, so Messer Nicolò sailed on to Constantinople, where he became embroiled in the endless feud within the ruling dynasty.

Emperor John V had been overthrown by his son Andronicus with the backing of the Genoese, but he had managed to escape from prison. Andronicus, meanwhile, had entrenched himself in Pera, the Genoese fortified citadel inside the city. Emperor John asked Messer Nicolò to help him capture his son and root out the rebels. At first Messer Nicolò resisted because he did not want to put his contingent at risk even before meeting up with his brother. But according to Chinazzo, the chronicler, after so many weeks at sea the men had "a strong desire to fight." So the Venetians stormed the citadel and put Emperor John back on the throne.

At the end of August, Messer Nicolò sailed back to Tenedos, where he finally met up with Carlo (along the way he raided two Genoese cogs heavy with caviar, leather, hemp, wax, silk and other precious goods brought down from the Sea of Azov). The combined fleet under Carlo's command, now numbering fifteen galleys, headed south and split up before reaching Cyprus. Carlo, at the head of twelve galleys, sailed to Syria to sell the goods he had in storage and load up with eastern merchandise before returning to Venice. Nicolò headed to Rhodes with the remaining three galleys. He was to stock up on food, wine and water and purchase "all the biscuit he could find" so that the fleet would be ready to return to Venice at the end of the summer.

In Rhodes, however, Messer Nicolò came upon the legendary *Bichignona,* the largest and richest cog the Genoese had ever put to sea and possibly the mightiest ship to sail in the Mediterranean during the fourteenth century. The "floating city," as she was known, was the most tantalizing prey, filled with terrified merchants huddling around a treasure worth half a million ducats. Her crew was no match for Messer Nicolò's battle-hardened swordsmen and bowmen. But, after unloading much of her rich cargo to lighten her weight, the *Bichignona* took advantage of an unfurling breeze to slip away from the three approaching Venetian galleys. Just as her lucky escape seemed assured, Carlo arrived on the scene with his twelve galleys. He immediately commandeered a Catalan cog anchored at Rhodes to provide cover for his men during the assault (a cog was higher than a galley) and took off after the huge Genoese ship. As long as the breeze held, the *Bichignona* was faster than the Venetian galleys; it set a northeastern course hoping to find even stronger winds in the Aegean. But seventy miles into her run the wind died and the Venetians were upon her, setting her sails on fire and unleashing a wave of quivering arrows against the merchants and soldiers crowding the Genoese ship. Twenty-four were killed in the attack; the Venetians lost only one man, although sixty were wounded. Among them was Carlo: an arrow pierced his foot and another opened a gash near one eye.

The booty was divided, and after the galley captains had taken their generous share each bowman received forty ducats and each oarsman received twenty. At last, in late October, as the first chills of autumn reached the southern Mediterranean, the much-invigorated fleet set sail toward the Adriatic to rescue Venice from the Genoese.

Carlo and Messer Nicolò arrived in the nick of time. During their absence, Doge Contarini had ventured out of Venice at the head of a battered fleet to lay siege to the Genoese anchored in Chioggia. The doge felt that the only way to delay a final attack on Venice was to besiege the besiegers; he was also buying time in the hope that the Zen brothers would arrive from the east with reinforcements. Ships and barges were loaded with stones and sunk in the shallow waters of the canals connecting Chioggia to the mainland and to the sea in order to block escape routes and supply lines. But the siege was not sustainable for long. The doge had very limited forces at his disposal. Most of the men at the oars were grumbling shopkeepers and artisans who had been forcibly recruited. By the time winter set in, pressure was mounting to withdraw back to Venice and hunker down in the lagoon. The arrival of Carlo's fifteen-galley fleet on January 1, 1381, gave the Venetians an enormous psychological boost and a strategic advantage that allowed them to tighten the noose around Chioggia. In June the worn-out Genoese surrendered. Five thousand prisoners were taken to Venice, where most of them were left to die of illness and malnutrition.

Carlo was given the command of the Venetian fleet and

began to clear the Adriatic of Genoese ships. Messer Nicolò was appointed *savio alla guerra,* secretary of war, and was then put in charge of Venice's land forces (*chapetano de gente e de campo*). Later in the year the Peace of Turin finally brought peace between the two Mediterranean rivals. Genoa never recovered its preeminence. Venice was victorious but exhausted and weak.

MANY VENETIAN merchants lost their fortunes during the war. Not so Messer Nicolò, who increased his wealth thanks to the plundering of the *Bichignona* and other wartime raids. According to the public record, he purchased the house of his impoverished next-door neighbor at San Fantin, the combined properties forming a substantial palazzo. Although I could not find a birth certificate that would tell me his exact age, my guess was that Messer Nicolò had reached fifty by the time the war was over. He barely had time to settle in with his family in their larger, more comfortable house before the Senate appointed him to a three-man delegation that was to travel to Ferrara to negotiate the new borders of Padua (one of Genoa's allies in the war) with the marquess of Este. In the autumn of 1381 he signed over power of attorney to two business associates, Remigio Soranzo and Vittorio Diedo, who were to look after his wife, Fantina, and their four children while he was away. However, Doge Contarini died and Messer Nicolò, together with the other two members of the delegation, stayed in Venice to participate in the election of the new doge, Michele Morosini. The diplomatic mission to Ferrara was postponed to the following year (1382).

Nicolò the Younger did not specify when Messer Nicolò sailed to Flanders except to say that it was after the war with the Genoese. But since I found no record of him at all in the archives for the period from 1383 to 1388, I imagine that he prepared his journey no earlier than the fall and winter of 1382–83 and sailed in the spring of 1383.

The Battle of Chioggia (1381) was the final turning point in the century-long war between Venice and Genoa for supremacy in the Mediterranean. Carlo Zen, aided by his brother Nicolò, played a decisive role in Venice's last-minute victory.

Romania and the Black Sea, the region he knew so well and that had made him a rich man, would have been a more obvious destination for Messer Nicolò than Flanders—a part of the world where, at least according to the available record, he had never sailed before. But in the aftermath of the war with Genoa, Venice was looking to reinvigorate its commercial empire, which had been largely dependent on the trade routes in the eastern Mediterranean. The growing markets in the northern seas offered attractive possibilities to Venetian merchants, especially now that the Genoese had been weakened.

Actually, Venice was not new to those markets. The Republic had started to send sea convoys to Flanders as early as the beginning of the fourteenth century, mainly to avoid the dangers and pitfalls of overland travel. Until then, Venetians wishing to bring their goods to the great market of Bruges had had to suffer grueling journeys across Europe during which they were oppressed by endless customs duties and constantly under threat from roadside bandits. The traveling itself, much of it over mountainous terrain, was physically exhausting as the roads were primitive and often flooded. Transactions had to be conducted in any number of incomprehensible idioms. As a result, Venetian trade with Western Europe had never really flourished. But with the introduction of round-bodied ships in the Mediterranean, a sea route to Flanders became an attractive alternative to land convoys. The journey was far less difficult, the ships carried bigger loads and the merchants were able to communicate in linguafranca, the simple, functional language that was spoken in all the ports of the Mediterranean and the Atlantic. It was made up of words from Portuguese, Catalan, Venetian, Genoese, Greek, Latin and Arabic and although there is no written record of this extraordinary idiom, it is known to have been the chosen means of communication among sailors and merchants in the Middle Ages and beyond.

There was, of course, another reason why Venetians began to sail to Flanders: they thrived at sea, and they preferred having to weather a storm or face the occasional assault by a pirate ship than slog their way along muddy European roads.

The first Venetian ships sailed to Flanders as early as 1313. Those first contacts were so promising that four years later Venice established a state-sponsored shipping line to the region, with the Senate leasing up to eight galleys to the highest bidders in its yearly auctions. The Venetians obtained important trading rights and guarantees from the local authorities in Bruges and opened a consulate in the city's market square to signal they were there to stay. Venetian state galleys were quite an intimidating sight, always traveling in convoy and heavily armed. The two-way journey lasted from four to six months. The government fixed the itinerary and listed the goods to be transported. Increasingly, Venice had come to view the Atlantic trade route as a new strategic component of its economy.

Each Venetian merchant ship traveling to the ports of England and Flanders (Bruges was usually the terminus of the line) was quite a sight to behold—a large floating emporium filled with the greatest variety of goods. Wine, paper, earthenware, glass, jewels, refined silks and other Venetian manufactured goods were in plentiful supply. The ships carried wax and leather from Romania, cotton from Egypt, hemp from Syria, as well as less obvious raw materials, such as crates of elephant tusks for the Flemish ivory artisans. And there was the usual load of sweet delicacies: brown sugar, candied fruits, currants, dried prunes, dates.

Most of the sacks in the hull, however, were stuffed with exotic herbs and roots. It was said of Venetian ships that they left such a profusion of pungent aromas in their wake at sea that they could be detected miles away given the right wind. The most common spices were ginger from Malabar, cinnamon from Ceylon, pepper from Hindustan, cloves from Egypt, nutmeg from Malacca and wormwood from Persia. Spices were intended for cooking but also for cosmetic and pharmaceutical purposes. Ginger, for example, was a precious stimulant and antiscorbutic. Gum arabic was a widely used astringent. Sal ammoniac was an effective sudorific. Galangal, a popular diuretic, also helped stimulate menstruation. Borax cured glandular and spleen diseases. Musk was an effective antidote to poison. Belzoe had a soothing effect on asthmatics. Turpentine was said to cure gonorrhea. A wide choice of purgatives was also available, from refined scammony, which was very strong, to milder remedies, such as rhubarb, manna and aloe. There were "uppers" and "downers": ambergris was used against melancholia and as a sexual stimulant; saffron and camphor had a tranquilizing effect and supposedly cured women of "hysterics."

One can imagine the relief with which those floating pharmacies, brimming with remedies for every possible ailment, were greeted in the northern countries.

DURING THE war with Genoa, the government-sponsored line to Flanders was of course interrupted. It was not reinstated until four years after the end of hostilities, in 1385. But Messer Nicolò was evidently anxious to leave because, according to Nicolò the Younger, he chose to "[build] and [equip] a ship with his own riches" rather than wait until he could lease a galley from the government. It was a riskier course to take because he would not have the protection afforded to a convoy; on the other hand, he would be free to chart his itinerary and set his schedule without having to abide by the restrictive rules established by the Venetian authorities.

Why so much haste on Messer Nicolò's part? Although one can only speculate about his reasons, I suspect he simply wanted to beat his competitors to the rich markets of England and Flanders after the crippling war against the Genoese. All his life he had been a restless merchant, always on the lookout for new commercial opportunities. The spread of Church influence during the late Middle Ages had vastly increased demand for dried and salted fish across

Europe. The cod and herring trade in the North Sea was booming and promised to be an important complement to the spice trade that dominated the traditional eastern routes Messer Nicolò knew so well.

The ship of choice for a merchant sailing on his own to Flanders in the fourteenth century, and the one Messer Nicolò most certainly used, was the cog—a round, bulky, one- or two-mast vessel with high battlements, a steep hull and a very deep hold that could carry a much more substantial cargo than the traditional galley. The ship, steered with a long axial rudder fixed to the poop frame, was stable and seaworthy; it plowed the deep swells of the Atlantic with a natural ease.

The cog originated in the northern seas and was widely used by the German merchants of the Hanseatic League before it appeared in the Mediterranean at the end of the thirteenth century. Venetians, who had used galleys for centuries, started converting to the cog in the early fourteenth century as they ventured beyond the Strait of Gibraltar. Although the cog was specifically designed to navigate in the Atlantic, it was soon widely used in the Mediterranean as well.

There are surprisingly few drawings of Venetian cogs in the Venice archives and I found the best way to get a sense of their size and shape was to look at those moored by the Rialto or in Saint Mark's Basin in the paintings by Carpaccio, the great narrative painter of the early Venetian Renaissance.

The cog had elegant, clean lines. It was built with Dalmatian oak and pinewood logged in the nearby Julian Alps and combined solidity with lightness. It was less expensive to run than a galley, as it carried fewer oarsmen—an average of sixty compared to two hundred. It could also hold more merchandise in relation to its size, a typical midsize cog carrying up to three to four hundred tons. It was more vulnerable to attack at sea, relying mostly on a small contingent of bowmen. But all men on board were expected to seize arms if the ship was under attack.

In Messer Nicolò's time, shipowners were also mounting fixed bombards on the cog's fore and aft decks, similar to those used for the first time by the Venetians during the siege of Chioggia. These were stout, stumpy cannons made of rope and wood pressed into a leather casing that was about twenty inches long and eight inches wide. Also on board were sleek, bazooka-like cannons cast in iron and used for shooting small rocks at the assailing enemy.

I pictured Messer Nicolò poring over charts of the Atlantic coast during the winter of 1382–83; gathering information on winds, tides and ports of call from veterans of the route to Flanders; storing merchandise in the capacious hull of his new ship that could be easily sold or exchanged for

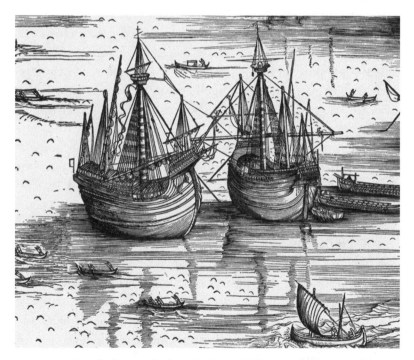

Nicolò Zen sailed to the Sea of Flanders in a cog,
or round ship, probably similar to the two seen
here anchored in the Basin of Saint Mark. Detail from
Jacopo de Barbari's view of Venice.

other goods; interviewing seamen, oarsmen, bowmen, carpenters and caulkers to take on board with him; stocking supplies for the journey: wine, cheese, salted pork, beans and a large quantity of *biscotto,* the heavily buttered wheat-flour biscuit that formed the basis of nutrition aboard Venetian ships (starting in 1335 the Republic began to mass-produce *biscotto* in government-run ovens).

There was one last delay. In May 1383, just as Messer Nicolò was getting ready to leave, the Senate nominated him ambassador to Hungary, an important and politically sensitive post. According to the rules, the appointee had to have enough money to support four servants, a notary and his assistant, two secretaries, a purser and a cook, and to spend an average of six ducats a day on general expenditures for his family. Messer Nicolò could easily have fulfilled those requirements, but evidently his mind was set on going back to sea. He declined the appointment and was fined one hundred ducats—a fairly standard sanction in such cases. He paid the fine and set sail most probably in early June.

The journey to Flanders took about two months. The government convoys usually stopped in Sicily, then crossed over to Majorca, and from there sailed to Málaga. But a private captain was not bound to follow that itinerary. Indeed, it would have been risky for him to make a crossing in open sea from Sicily all the way to Majorca. The choice was either to sail north, follow the southern coast of France and then go down the coast of Spain, with stops for provisions in Marseille, Barcelona, Valencia and Málaga, or else to take the southern route to the Barbary Coast, with stops in Tunis, Tangier and Málaga. He would then sail through the Strait of Gibraltar and along the Bay of Cádiz, round Cape St. Vincent and head north to Lisbon.

Messer Nicolò was of course familiar with navigation in the Mediterranean, but according to the records in the Venice Archives he had never ventured into the Atlantic before. The aim of any captain heading to Flanders was to stay close to shore and follow the Atlantic coastline of Portugal around Cape Finisterre, sail along Asturias and Cantabria in the Bay of Biscay and then head north all the way up to the craggy, treacherous coast of Brittany. Aboard his ship, he would have had a limited number of instruments to help him stay on course, the most important being the thirty-two-point magnetic compass that was commonly used by Venetian merchants in the fourteenth century, and charts describing local coastlines, harbors, sheltered coves and danger zones. In any case, sailing north against the current and the powerful trade winds was bound to be rough on a loaded Venetian cog.

As Messer Nicolò and his men rounded Brittany and entered the English Channel, navigation became more difficult. Choppy seas, steep waves, frequent fog and shifting sandbars: even an experienced old salt like Messer Nicolò must have felt he was advancing into a hostile environment. The tides were far more powerful than anything he had seen in the Mediterranean; they created deep currents and surface currents that changed direction every six hours and made it even more difficult to stay on course.

Stormy weather was frequent in the early summer and a magnetic compass would have been useless in such conditions. And with the skies heavy with clouds not even the stars could have rescued Messer Nicolò when, according to Nicolò the Younger's narrative, he lost his bearings somewhere in the Sea of Flanders. "He was caught in a fierce storm and drifted for many days, tossed by waves and winds until he no longer knew where he was; at last he sighted land and unable to fight the awful tempest any further, he hit the shore of Frislanda."

CHAPTER THREE

Frislanda

A FTER MANY days and nights adrift in a hostile sea, Messer Nicolò and his exhausted crew caught sight of looming dark mountains surging through the watery mist. For all their relief at the approaching land, they must have felt in awe of the dramatic scene that suddenly opened up to them. The islands, tall and angular, were separated from one another by narrow, deep-water fjords. Black cliffs cut into the freezing sea. Waterfalls dropped from the uplands, crashing into the ocean swell. Low, fast-moving clouds enhanced the eerie atmosphere surrounding these remote and lonely islands.

After steering through a barrier of treacherous outcroppings, "Messer Nicolò landed with all his men alive and most of the goods safe." They clambered out of their battered cog, dazed and stiff-limbed. But before they were able to get their bearings and set up camp on the rocky shore they were surrounded by a crowd of threatening, shouting men armed with axes and picks and stones. Weakened by dehydration and malnourishment after so many days at sea, they stood little chance of surviving an attack. Nicolò the Younger, always quick to praise his countrymen's valor, conceded "they were unlikely to put up a vigorous defense and would have been harshly dealt with had good fortune not come their way."

Good fortune appeared in the form of a "prince"—a lord and commander who, alerted by the news of the rough land-

*The mysterious island of Frislanda drawn by Nicolò Zen
the Younger on the* Carta da navegar *published by
Francesco Marcolini in 1558.*

ing, rode his horse to the scene and quickly ordered his men
to scatter the mob of natives. The prince addressed Messer
Nicolò in Latin and, upon learning that he came from
Venice, reacted with *"grandissima allegrezza"*—the greatest
joy. He offered the bedraggled Venetians his protection and
assured them they would be treated well.

At first I found the scene described by Nicolò the
Younger somewhat hard to believe—the mysterious prince
bursting into effusive gestures of friendship upon hearing
that Messer Nicolò hailed from Venice. But even though
these two men clearly belonged to worlds that were very far
apart, they may well have had more in common than I had
initially imagined. The prince's ability to communicate in

Latin suggested he was a well-born, cultivated man; as such, he would indeed have been familiar with the Venetian Republic. Venice was, after all, the great naval power of the time, and news of its historic victory over the Genoese had certainly traveled very far north by the time Messer Nicolò reached Frislanda. Also, in the high Middle Ages Venice served as the gateway to the Holy Land. It was the duty of every good Christian to make a pilgrimage to Jerusalem at least once in his lifetime, and the great majority of those who actually made the journey traveled to Venice from all over Europe, and there they boarded the transport ships that took them across the Mediterranean. An educated nobleman like the prince would have contemplated a journey via Venice to the Holy Land—indeed, he could well have already made it.

NICOLÒ THE Younger claimed the prince's name was Zichmni—a bizarre combination of phonemes, which, as far as I could tell, had no recognizable etymology. It was probably the result of a wrong transcription from one of the original letters sent home by Messer Nicolò. Zichmni's true identity remains controversial, as we shall see. But Nicolò the Younger did provide two significant clues: Zichmni was "lord of Sorant, a region near Scotland," and he ruled over "a group of islands named Porlanda, to the south of Frislanda, which were the richest and most populous in the entire region."

Zichmni, it turned out, was in Frislanda on a military expedition to quash a rebellion on the part of the natives. He wasted little time in drafting the Venetians to his cause, instructing Messer Nicolò to join the flotilla anchored in the bay (a cog, two longships and ten barks) and to advise the captain on how best to seize control of several smaller islands in the archipelago.

Nicolò the Younger noted with patriotic pride that "Zichmni quickly understood Messer Nicolò was not only wise but very experienced in seafaring matters." Drawing on the original material, Nicolò the Younger went on to describe in some detail a two-pronged military operation to seize control of Frislanda: "While Zichmni led one contingent cross-country, the small fleet carrying the Venetians sailed west and easily took two outlying islands, Ledovo and Ilofe. The ships then turned toward the Gulf of Sudero and weighed anchor in the village of Sanestol, where they came upon several vessels loaded with salted fish. In Sanestol, they were briefly joined by Zichmni's forces, which had marched across the main island of Frislanda. Then the fleet sailed to the north of the Gulf of Sudero and after taking control of a few more islets, anchored at Bondendon, a fishing village at the west end of the fjord."

Nicolò the Younger claimed the contribution of the small Venetian contingent was decisive. "The sea in which they had navigated was so filled with reefs," he wrote, "that the fleet would have been lost had it not been for Messer Nicolò and his mariners; the other men were less experienced than ours, for whom the art of navigation was second nature." Of course Nicolò the Younger had a habit of glorifying Venetian prowess in battle, but how naïve to think that his countrymen would be more adept at sailing in those treacherous fjords than local seamen!

At Bondendon, Messer Nicolò and his men learned that Zichmni had completed his campaign victoriously. Nicolò the Younger went on to write, "First the rebel chiefs came to lay down their arms and submit to his authority. Then Zichmni himself arrived and there was much joy and jubilation for the victories on land and those at sea, for which the Venetians in particular were celebrated. In fact one only heard praise for them and for Messer Nicolò's great valor. The prince greatly admired courageous men, especially those who were well versed in the art of seafaring. He summoned Messer Nicolò and after praising his skill and ingenuity, and paying tribute to the important role he had played in pre-

serving the fleet intact and subjugating so much territory
with little effort, he knighted him."

Such a rush to knight Messer Nicolò sounded to me a little suspect—Zichmni probably did so at a later date. But
knight him he did: Messer Nicolò kept the title after his
return to Venice a few years later. In most of the family trees
I found in the archives he was generally referred to as
Nicolò, il Kavaliere—Nicolò the Chevalier.

The Frislanda Enigma

NICOLÒ THE YOUNGER was the first to write about
Frislanda and to draw a map of it—there are no traces of
such an island on earlier European charts or travel narratives. Evidently his reputation and his social rank were solid
enough that this large island he placed with so much confidence to the north of Scotland soon found its way onto the
major maps of the sixteenth century. But of course there
was no such island where he had placed it, so I wondered
where Messer Nicolò and his men could have made their
landfall.

Geographers long before me had scratched their heads
over this question. When mariners reported they could not
find Frislanda some began to think that Nicolò the Younger
had made the whole story up; most, however, took the view
that the island had probably been submerged by a volcanic
explosion since the days of Messer Nicolò. It was not until
1787 that a French geographer, Jean Nicolas Buache, asserted
in a scholarly article, "*Mémoire sur l'isle de Frislande*," that
while Frislanda as depicted in the Zen map did not exist, the
latitude of the island in the chart (roughly 62°) indicated
Nicolò the Younger was probably describing the Faroes.
Five years later, a German geographer, von Eggers, came to
the same conclusion after identifying a number of place-
names on the map of Frislanda that corresponded to place-

names in the Faroes: Monaco for Munk, Sudero for Sutheroy (Suðeroy), Nordero for Northedalur (Norðadalur), Andeford for Arnafjord (Arnafjørður), to name a few.* Other writers weighed in and by the early nineteenth century it was generally agreed that Frislanda was in fact a deformed and enlarged representation of the Faroes.

It seemed to me a reasonable enough solution to the riddle. In Viking days this remote archipelago in the North Atlantic was known as Faerøeisland, the Islands of the Sheep. It was easy to imagine how Messer Nicolò, writing home at the end of the fourteenth century, might have contracted and Italianized the old Viking name from Faerøeisland to Frislanda.

A hundred and fifty years later, Nicolò the Younger, who was neither a geographer nor a cartographer, worked from the scraps of letters and the chart he had found in Palazzo Zen to trace the outline of Frislanda. Contrary to his claim that it "came out rather well," as he wrote, quite pleased with himself, he did a terrible job of it, soldering the narrow islands that form the archipelago into a single, supersized landmass that hadn't the faintest resemblance to the actual Faroes. He made matters worse by placing his fanciful Frislanda at the correct latitude, as Buache pointed out, but in the wrong position relative to other important pieces of the North Atlantic puzzle: Shetland, Iceland and Greenland.

Clearly, the letters and chart Nicolò the Younger used were not the only source of his Frislanda. At least one existing map is sure to have inspired him, and to have led him further astray. It is the map of another nonexistent island in the North Atlantic called Fixlanda (the Island of Fish), which

---

* The Faroese and Icelandic languages use an extended Latin alphabet with characters that do not exist in English. Some place-names are common enough that there is a standard English transliteration, but other places in this book are so rarely mentioned in English that there is no usual Anglicization. In those cases, for ease of reading, I have given the name in its native language on the first use, and used my own transliteration throughout.

Matteo Prunes, a cartographer from Majorca, published in 1553, five years before the Zen map came out. As many as thirteen of the twenty place-names in Prunes's Fixlanda appear on Frislanda in one form or another, suggesting Nicolò the Younger took a good long peek at it before drawing his own map.*

Nicolò the Younger was later accused of having taken some of his information for the Zen map from the *Carta marina* (1539), a famous map by Olaus Magnus, a Swedish bishop who sought refuge in Italy after the Reformation, and which was considered at the time to be the most up-to-date depiction of the North Atlantic. I found it a curious charge: in the *Carta marina* the Faroes are traced quite accurately and there is no Frislanda. If Nicolò the Younger consulted Olaus's map—and it would have been easily available to him in Venice—he evidently did not think it was very reliable. Indeed, by inserting Frislanda with such assurance in his outline of the North Atlantic and by erasing the Faroes altogether, he must have thought his map a great step forward relative to the *Carta marina.* Certainly many of his contemporaries believed it to be the case, judging by the influence the Zen map had in shaping the sixteenth-century view of the North Atlantic.

Noregsveldi

The Faroes are a dramatic sight—they surge from the abyss halfway between Shetland and Iceland to form one last anchorage before the vast expanse of the North Atlantic.

---

* These are (the place-names on the Prunes map are in parentheses): Porlanda (Porlanda), Sanestol (Sunifise), C. deria (C. deviya), Porti (Porti), Cabaru (Caruo), Spagia (Espraya), Aqua (Aqua), Forali (Forasi), Campa (Compo), Rodea (Radeal), Dossais (Dorasais), Godmec (Godinech), Sorand (Solanda). The source of the Prunes map, in turn, was probably a fifteenth-century Catalan chart depicting Fixlanda.

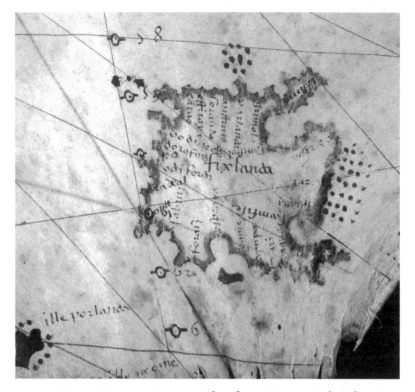

*Mateo Prunes, a cartographer from Majorca, placed
Fixlanda to the northwest of the British Isles in his 1553
nautical chart. Fixlanda may well have served as a model
for Nicolò Zen the Younger's Frislanda five years later.*

Several million years ago, an incandescent mass emerged
amid thrashing, churning waters and quickly hardened, giving shape to a dozen elongated islands, set one next to the
other along a northwest/southeast axis and separated by
long, narrow sea arms. The fallout from successive volcanic
eruptions built up great layer cakes of lava and turf that are
covered with a sprinkling of emerald green.

Even today the approach to these beautiful islands in the
middle of the ocean can be as intimidating as it must have
been in the time of Messer Nicolò. The Faroes are often

shrouded in mist, gales blow hard and ominous grey swells crash furiously against the black rocks. At first sight, it can seem a bleak and lonely world. But then the sun will suddenly break out through the mist, unveiling a vivid, gentler landscape. Sheep graze placidly on the uplands; old farmsteads, their roofs covered with turf and brilliant grass, stand peacefully in generous meadows; and brightly painted fishing villages give an occasional spot of color to the coastline.

Hardy monks from Ireland were the first to reach these islands, in the early part of the eighth century. They came in hide-covered *currachs,* carrying only a few sheep and other bare essentials, to find a solitary place where they could pray and feel close to God. When the Vikings escaping the tyranny of King Harald Finehair landed in the Faroes in the early ninth century, they found a few old hermits still living in caves; they called them *papar,* "little fathers." The new settlers built homesteads, raised sheep and fished. They traded wool and cod for corn, timber, glass, amber beads and soapstone brought over by merchant ships from the Norwegian mainland. The sagas tell us it was a peaceful community governed by local chieftains. But the expanding kingdom of Norway—the Noregsveldi—absorbed the Faroes in 1035 under King Magnus the Good.

By the time Messer Nicolò's ship was storm driven into the region three and a half centuries later, the overextended Noregsveldi was losing influence. The Faroes, like other sea dominions of the realm, were in turmoil. The tax-collecting system had broken down. Trade had dwindled to a trickle. Pirates raided the farmsteads and the churches. And the ruthless sea merchants of the Hanseatic League lurked in Faroese waters looking to take over the profitable cod market. When young Queen Margaret succeeded her husband King Haakon in 1380 she faced the daunting task of preserving the Crown's authority not only in the Faroes, but in Orkney and in Shetland, in distant Iceland and in the remotest dominions of all, the half-forgotten colonies in Greenland.

This was the world Messer Nicolò and his men drifted into, in the summer of 1383: a legendary sea empire in rapid decline.

I KNEW very little about the Faroes apart from what I had gleaned from a few books I had taken out from the library in Venice. The temptation to visit those remote islands in my quest to find further traces of the Zen saga proved irresistible. I booked an airplane ticket from London Gatwick to the Faroes on Atlantic Airways, the Faroese national carrier.

Landing in the Faroes can be a hair-raising affair. The airstrip, originally built by the British during World War II, lies in a meadow atop Vágar, the third largest island of the archipelago. The weather conditions are often hazardous and the aircraft can be forced to turn back. I was lucky to arrive on a clear evening. The plane circled over the crest of the mountain like a wide-winged seabird looking for a perch in the middle of the ocean; it landed quickly and gracefully, and came to a halt just before reaching the cliffs.

A sleek bus took me down to sea-level and then through a long tunnel that connected Vágar to Streymoy, the main island. As I soon discovered, the larger islands, although separated by deep fjords, were linked by an integrated, high-tech transportation system: fast ferries, helicopters and, impressively, a series of deep sea tunnels—engineering marvels paid for by the Danish government. The integration of this futuristic infrastructure with the pristine Faroese environment appeared seamless. I half expected to see James Bond's Aston Martin zoom by and disappear into the landscape.

Tórshavn (population 17,500), the capital of the Faroes, is named after the Norse thunder god, Thor. It is a small harbor town set in the bay where, in Viking days, the Faroese chiefs used to meet for their yearly assembly. The waterfront is lined with brightly colored buildings; behind them a knot of winding streets untangles itself in front of small detached houses, their roofs covered with rich, grassy turf that keeps out the dampness.

I quickly settled into a pleasant routine. Every morning I walked the length of the harbor from my hotel over to the National Library and worked there until lunchtime, pulling out books from the shelves and sifting through old texts on the medieval history of the Faroes. The National Archives and the University of the Faroe Islands were housed in a small cluster of buildings nearby, so it was easy to walk from one to the other and arrange meetings with local historians and archivists over a cup of coffee. The few who had heard about the Zen story invariably dismissed it as the handiwork of a two-bit Venetian swindler.

In the afternoons, I drove along the fjords and up the mountains and disappeared into sea tunnels that went down to the bottom of the ocean. After dinner, I stopped by the Café Natur, a favorite hangout, to watch the local scene and sip Faroese beer before returning to my hotel. The young people wore funky, fashionable clothes. They rode their motorbikes without helmets and sprinkled their Faroese sentences with English words like "yeah," "thanks" and "good-bye."

The first thing I learned was how much the Faroese yearned to regain the independence they lost way back in early medieval times, when they were absorbed into the Norse realm. Denmark granted the Faroes self-government in 1948 but most Faroese I spoke to said it was not enough. "We will soon become a sovereign nation within the European Union," Magni Arge, the visionary boss of Atlantic Airways, confidently predicted to me late one night over beers at Café Natur.

I asked Arge how he thought such a tiny country lost in the ocean could possibly survive on its own. He sketched the plan of a vibrant island economy based on the fishing industry, sheep farming and tourism. Besides, he said, the Faroese already possessed many of the trappings of a sovereign nation. They had a language, which was very similar to the old language of the Vikings because the remoteness of the islands had limited its contamination. They had a stable currency, the Faroese króna. They had a flag (a red Scandinavian cross with a blue edge against a white background). They had a national university and a national library and a small national museum, housed in a refitted farm by the sea just a short walk out of Tórshavn.

"We also have a national soccer team," Arge said with a grin, and went on to describe an epic battle during the qualifying rounds for the 1992 European Championship, during which a band of plucky Faroese upstarts managed to hold the mighty Danish team to a tie until the end of the first half. "I remember feeling for the first time that we had truly come together as one nation," he added with unexpected gravitas.

That year Denmark had the strongest team in Europe. It went on to trounce the Faroese side during the second half with a final score of 4 to 1, and eventually took the championship.

I knew something about the Faroese team. Years later Italy, then the reigning world champion, was scheduled to play against the Faroes in a qualifying game for the European Championship. I remembered reading in the newspaper at the time about the Italians' harrowing attempts to land on the airstrip at Vágar. They finally made it, but, still shaken from the trip, they barely managed to edge out the Faroese on the wet soccer field just outside Tórshavn.

It seemed to me that despite the great strides the Faroes had made on the road to independence, the sheer remoteness of these islands would continue to be a serious handicap. "At this point," the ever-buoyant Arge insisted, "all we really need to make it on our own is a successful national air carrier. Running the airline on a daily basis can sometimes turn into a scheduling nightmare because of the weather conditions, but my goal is to put the Faroes at the center of air traffic in the North Atlantic." And with that, he pulled out from his briefcase a map of the North Atlantic that stretched from Newfoundland to Scandinavia. The Faroes were indeed at the very center of the map—a tiny speck in the middle of the ocean out of which surged a busy fountain of airline trajectories to London, Copenhagen, Reykjavik and even faraway Nuuk, the capital of Greenland.

ARGE WAS enthusiastic about the Zen voyages. He liked the connection it established between Venice and the Faroes. "You should go see my friend Jóannes Patursson over in Kirkjubøur [Arge pronounced it *Cheech-bahr*]. It's at the tip of the Sutheroy Fjord, where your Venetians did battle. You'll like it there. Jóannes's farmhouse is the oldest in the Faroes."

I had read that Kirkjubøur, meaning "Church-farm," was once the largest community in the Faroes. The first bishop arrived there around AD 1100, a hundred years after the islands converted to Christianity. He built a sturdy little church of dark volcanic stone in a meadow by the edge of the water. His house, next to the church, was made with heavy logs brought over from Norway. The township prospered thanks to its rich pastures and fishing grounds. By the end of the twelfth century there were as many as seventy to eighty homesteads—more than a thousand people. Among them was an ambitious young priest by the name of Sverre Sigurdsson. One day he sailed to Norway and seized power at the head of the Birkebeiners, rebels who were so named for their rough shoes of birch bark.

King Sverre ruled Norway from 1184 to 1202 and went down in history as one of the great Norse kings—which I thought was not entirely surprising since *Sverre's Saga* was written under his supervision. The decline of Kirkjubøur in the fourteenth century coincided with the decline of the Norse kingdom. At the time of Messer Nicolò's forced landing in 1383, the township had probably lost some of its importance. Still, I was a little surprised not to find any mention at all of Kirkjubøur in Nicolò the Younger's narrative, or at least of a place-name vaguely resembling it.

It was when I heard Arge pronounce it *Cheech-bahr* that it suddenly occurred to me that Kirkjubøur was probably the town of Ocibar (*oh-chee-bahr*), which Nicolò the Younger had placed on the southern coast of Frislanda on the Zen map. Next to the name was a decorative marker: a steeple surrounded by several buildings, indicating this was a township of some standing as well as a religious center.

I had been intrigued from the start by Ocibar because that place-name did not appear on any other existing map, including the Prunes map, and I had concluded that Nicolò the Younger could only have found it on a chart of the Faroese coastline sent by Messer Nicolò to his brothers in Venice.

I took Arge's advice and drove out to Kirkjubøur to pay Jóannes a visit. The road wound its way up into the mountains behind Tórshavn. On the uplands, the mist dissolved and I had a sweeping view of the Sutheroy Fjord: Koltur and Hestur rising high to my right; Sandoy straight ahead across the fjord and Sutheroy, the last of the Faroes, on the southern horizon.

If Sutheroy Fjord was indeed the Gulf of Sudero of the Zen narrative, then it followed that the seascape spread out before me was the theater of those naval operations in which Messer Nicolò and the Venetians participated after their rough landing. I knew it made little sense to try to trace the course of action described in the book. But as I stood on the edge of the road taking in the view, I could not help wondering whether the small port of Sandur on the island of Sandoy, which I could see straight ahead of me, might not be the village of Sanestol, where Messer Nicolò came upon those fishing boats laden with cod—boats, I now realized, that must surely have belonged to Hanseatic merchants, the only ones licensed by the Norwegian Crown to trade with the Faroes. And turning my gaze toward the west end of the fjord, where the old port of Norðadalur glimmered in the pale sunshine, it occurred to me that it might once have been the port of Bondendon (*bodden,* I knew, meant "the head of the bay"), where, "following the advice of Messer Nicolò, the captain anchored the fleet and waited for news of Zichmni's overland campaign."

From a military point of view, that campaign could not have amounted to much. Nicolò the Younger claimed that Zichmni "conquered the enemy after a great battle and seized all the land and all the fortified cities." But at the time, the Faroese population probably did not amount to five thousand souls in the entire archipelago. They had primitive weapons made of sticks and stones, and according to local historians there was very little by way of fortifications to be stormed. What Nicolò the Younger called "Zichmni's war" was more likely a large-scale police operation—a display of force intended to intimidate the Faroese, bring them to pay their taxes and accept the rule of the new queen Margaret.

I continued on to Kirkjubøur, driving down to the sea and then along the coastline, until I came to the end of the road. It was late afternoon. The Sutheroy Fjord was calm as a lake. The light had sharpened. Strands of golden kelp shimmered near the shore. It was a beautiful spot, and very peaceful.

The village of Kirkjubøur turned out to be no more than a cluster of farmhouses, all part of the same homestead— solid buildings made of good Norwegian timber, painted black with red trim and, as always, thick grass growing on the roof. Near the farmhouses, overlooking the fjord, stood the remains of an old church, its roof missing but all four walls still standing.

Jóannes Patursson, a sheep farmer in his early forties, greeted me with a friendly nod when I caught up with him at his farmhouse at the end of his work day. He had four hundred Faroese sheep grazing on the uplands. "Enough to get by," he said laconically.

Faroese sheep, this much I knew, hadn't changed much since Viking days: they were a frugal, tough-going breed and could stay out to pasture year-round because a thick layer of coarse dark hair protected them from the sleet and the rain and the snow.

"But underneath, the wool is soft and good for weaving," Jóannes said, lighting a cigarette and turning his gaze out to the sea. "It has a lot of lanolin."

Like his father, his grandfather and all his forefathers going back seventeen generations, Jóannes was born and raised in Kirkjubøur, and had lived there all his life—except for a brief stint in Australia, where he had gone as a young man to learn the little he didn't already know about sheep farming.

The Patursson clan came to the Faroes from Denmark right after the Reformation and took over all the land around Kirkjubøur. Jóannes still owned a small portion of that land and the few remaining farmhouses.

The main house on the homestead, where Jóannes lived with his family, was said to be a thousand years old. But he and his wife Guðrið had fixed up the interior like a New York loft, with waxed wooden floors, large windows, wide spaces and an open kitchen. Jóannes showed me around while two-year-old Rókur, the youngest of their four sons, played on the floor and Guðrið prepared meat sauce for the lasagne she planned to serve for their family dinner.

The old bishop's house was, literally, attached to the Paturssons' farmhouse. Jóannes explained to me that the original bishop's house had been built farther down the slope, on the edge of the water. But in the seventeenth century a tidal wave ripped across Sutheroy Fjord and tore up half the village of Kirkjubøur. All the houses closest to the sea were destroyed, including the bishop's. Of course by then Kirkjubøur had long ceased to be a diocese of the Church and there hadn't been a bishop in residence for many years. But the Patursson family rebuilt the house anyway, higher up, on dry land, close to their main farmhouse. So close, in fact, that the two houses now seemed part of the same building.

"Come with me," Jóannes said, leading me through a back door directly into the old bishop's house. It was dark and cavernous. The ceiling, very low, was supported by huge Norwegian logs that were at least three feet in diameter. Jóannes had transformed the main room into a rudimentary museum. A collection of objects he had dug up in the fields over the years, or fished out of the sea, was displayed haphazardly on several dusty shelves. I noticed a number of medieval fishing implements, as well as several combs made of whalebone, old pieces of cloth, a corroded knife and other domestic utensils, and a rusty cannonball the size of a clenched fist.

As he led me along, carefully pointing out each object, Jóannes took on a bemused expression, as if he were showing me pieces of a puzzle he had never been able to work out.

We left the bishop's house through the back door and walked over to the ruins of the church of Saint Magnus. A series of tie-rods had been placed on one side to prevent one of the walls from collapsing. "I cannot afford to restore it but I do what I can to preserve what is still standing," Jóannes said.

It was a large rectangular structure, standing against the sea like a shoebox without a lid. According to the old chronicles, around AD 1300 a bishop by the name of Erlend imposed an extra round of taxes on the overburdened Faroese to build this big church. This touched off a wave of popular protests across the archipelago. At the time of the uprising, Bishop Erlend was traveling in Norway and, fearing for his life, never returned to the Faroes. The church was therefore left unfinished. A hundred years later, Erik of Pomerania, king of Denmark, financed its completion. It must have been an impressive sight—such a grand church standing sentinel on the southern tip of Streymoy.

After the Reformation, the church was closed down. The rich wall-hangings, the finely carved pews, the gold goblets, the silver calices and reliquaries—everything of value was shipped to Denmark, which had succeeded Norway as the

Faroes' mother country as a result of dynastic changes in the fifteenth century.

"They stripped the place down," Jóannes observed. "Eventually the roof caved in and came crashing down. But the walls are very sturdy and have resisted well during the last six hundred years."

An evening breeze had picked up and was now blowing gently through the portal of the roofless church, the brackish air from the sea mixing with the smell of damp grass. We walked back to the farmhouse. The lasagne was sizzling in the baking pan and looked very crisp on the surface.

"Stay for dinner," Jóannes offered kindly, on his way to fetch a few cold bottles of beer.

During the meal, I explained to Jóannes and Guðrið what had brought me to the Faroes and expressed the view that, according to the place-names in the narrative by Nicolò the Younger, the naval operations he described in the book could well have occurred in the stretch of sea that was right before us.

Although he knew nothing of the Zen story, Jóannes did not react with surprise. "There was considerable activity in this area. I can feel it very strongly. But no one really knows what happened during most of the fourteenth century," he said. "At times," he said wistfully, "I feel someone came here and shut off all the lights."

An expert diver, Jóannes said he often searched for clues about the past in the dark and murky waters of Sutheroy Fjord, only to reemerge with some mysterious fragment or other that usually ended up gathering dust on a shelf in the old bishop's house.

But vestiges come in many different forms, and they will sometimes surface in the most unexpected ways.

THE DAY after my drive out to Kirkjubøur I stopped by Jacobsens Bookstore, in downtown Tórshavn, where I'd made a habit of dropping by. Most books were in Faroese and therefore incomprehensible to me. But I was drawn there by the intriguing notion that a tiny country with a population of 50,000 could sustain a thriving book industry, with a notable range—thrillers, historical novels, essays, poetry. One obvious reason was that the Faroese read a lot of Faroese books. Another was that local publishers had no distribution costs. There was only one outlet in all the Faroes: Jacobsens Bookstore.

I was browsing in the store when I chanced upon a book with an intriguing title in Latin, *Adventus Domini* (*The Advent of the Lord*). It was by a local author, Jógvan Isaksen, who taught Faroese literature at the University of Copenhagen. I leafed casually through the book until I was startled to find, among the illustrations, a full replica of the Zen map.

Adventus Domini belonged, this much I could guess, to the trendy category known in the trade as the Nordic thriller. A kindly customer helped me piece together the book's cockamamie plot, which went something like this:

Hannis Martinsson, a private detective in Tórshavn, is called in to investigate the murder of Bertie Angleton, a high official of the Order of Malta, killed while on his way to the farmstead in Kirkjubøur. Martinsson goes to see the farmer, who tells him the strange story of Messer Nicolò, a Venetian who had come to the Faroes in the fourteenth century to hide a rich treasure brought back from the Holy Land (it included the thirty silver pieces Judas received for betraying Jesus Christ). Messer Nicolò had specified in his will that if ever the story of his secret journey to the Faroes should come to light, the descendants of the farmer who had helped him hide the treasure should be informed about it. And so it was that after the publication of his book in 1558, Nicolò the Younger dutifully sent a copy to the family in Kirkjubøur, with a cover letter revealing the truth about Messer Nicolò's mission. Flash forward four and a half centuries: the farmer pulls out the dusty book and the Zen map and hands them to Detective Martinsson. Bertie Angleton had come to claim the treasure for the Order of Malta. But as the reader eventually discovers, the secret Order of the Templars has its eyes on it as well.

The author of *Adventus Domini* had Messer Nicolò hide the treasure in the wall of the old church at Kirkjubøur. I could not resist placing a call to Jóannes before leaving Tórshavn. He told me he knew about the book but had not read it and had never met the author.

"What about the treasure?" I asked. "The book says it was hidden in the wall of the church."

Jóannes laughed at the other end of the line. "My grandfather did find a box buried in a hole in the wall. It's still there. As far as I know it contains some relics of Saint Magnus."

CHAPTER FOUR

Zichmni

AFTER LOADING the ships with supplies, Zichmni and his men headed home "triumphantly," taking the newly knighted Messer Nicolò and the Venetians along with them. They sailed in a southeasterly direction and eventually reached an island that was "set in such a way as to form a great number of gulfs." The small fleet entered one of the wider ones and Messer Nicolò saw it was teeming with fish, for everywhere he looked, fishermen were "hauling copious catches" onto cargo ships bound for the great markets of Flanders, England and the Norse countries. Zichmni's boats proceeded toward the shore until "the principal city of the island" at last came into view.

At this tantalizing moment, Nicolò the Younger interrupted the description of their arrival, and I was left with the impression that he had given all the details he had been able to glean from an old and damaged letter in his hands. The scene dissolved into a blur even before the ships reached the harbor and the Venetians could disembark and take stock of their new surroundings. Lost in the rising fog, I wondered where it was that Messer Nicolò and his men had actually arrived.

Nicolò the Younger added to the confusion by stating that the name of this faceless city was also Frislanda; on the map, he placed it on the eastern coast of the island of Frislanda. This was not in itself surprising: Renaissance cartographers often gave towns they were not familiar with the name of the region. Some contemporary scholars have taken this to mean that Zichmni's fleet sailed to today's Tórshavn. But in medieval times there was not even a village where Tórshavn now stands, let alone a large and busy harbor at the center of a flourishing fishing trade. Besides, it didn't make sense to me that they should depart "triumphantly" from the scene of their campaign (Sutheroy Fjord) only to sail a few miles up the coast (Tórshavn).

I realized Zichmni himself, more than Nicolò the Younger, might help me discover the city where he had taken Messer Nicolò and the rest of the Venetians. But who *was* this Latin-speaking lord of Sorant and ruler of Porlanda "whose great valor and goodness," the narrative said, "made him as worthy of immortal memory as any man who ever lived"?

NICOLÒ THE Younger, this much was clear, had no idea. And no one bothered to find out for two hundred and some years following the publication of his book. Geographers in the sixteenth and seventeenth centuries were obviously more interested in places than people. It was only in 1786 that a Scots-Prussian naturalist by the name of John Reinhold Forster came up with a solution to the puzzle, which, despite its detractors, seems to have weathered the test of time.

Forster earned a footnote in the history of exploration by joining James Cook on his voyage to the Pacific aboard the *Resolution.* He was considered by his shipmates to be something of a pedant but he was endlessly curious, methodical and hard-working. After his return from the South Seas, he developed an interest in the history of cartography and became absorbed by the Zen voyages. While "employed on the subject," to use his own words, he was "struck by the conjecture" that Zichmni might be Henry Sinclair, earl of Orkney and lord of Rosslyn.

This Henry Sinclair was an ambitious Scotsman who lived at Rosslyn Castle, in the Esk Valley (Midlothian). He managed to leverage his family ties to the Norwegian Crown to gain influence in the Norse region at the end of the fourteenth century, around the time of Messer Nicolò's arrival. According to Forster, "Zichmni" was a mistaken transcription of "Sinclair," which was often spelled "Zincler" in the vernacular.

Not everyone agreed. Jakob Hornemann Bredsdorff, a Danish geographer, thought "Zichmni" was a distortion of "Sigmund," nephew of his better-known namesake Sigmund Bresterson, hero of the *Færeyinga Saga.* Another Danish writer, Father Krarup, claimed Henry de Siggens, marshal of the duke of Holstein's army, was the real Zichmni. And the English critic Frederick Lucas asserted Zichmni "far more closely resembles Wichmannus," a pirate described by Pontanus in his *Rerum danicarum historia,* whose "armed ships infested the shores and ports of Germany, France, Spain, Britain, Norway and Denmark." But none of these alternatives gathered much support beyond that of their respective authors, and by the nineteenth century most historians and geographers were inclined to believe that Zichmni was indeed Henry Sinclair.

I too felt the clues in the Zen narrative corroborated Forster's proposition. "Sorant" sounded to me like a contraction of "Sutherland," the northernmost county in mainland Scotland, where Henry Sinclair owned land. True, Nicolò the Younger writes that it was a region "near Scotland" rather than "in Scotland," but I considered this a minor, excusable error (perhaps less excusable was the fact that he then set the place-name Sorand on his map of Frislanda).

Even more significant was the indication that Zichmni "ruled over Porlanda, the richest and most populous islands in the region." This particular place-name was very probably derived from "Pomona," which was the old name for Mainland, Orkney's largest island. And the Orkney Islands were, unmistakably, the richest and most populous islands in the region.

In sum, I thought the reference to Sorant and Porlanda

underscored Zichmni's relationship to both Scotland and
Orkney and strengthened Forster's claim. And I was com-
forted by the fact that the biographer of the earls of Orkney,
Dr. Barbara Crawford of the University of Saint Andrews,
had also concluded as recently as the 1970s that "a natural
corruption of [the name] Sinclair [was] the most obvious"
solution to the Zichmni enigma.

I seized on it with relief. Forster's "conjecture" was no
proof that Zichmni was in fact Henry Sinclair, but the temptation to latch on to a figure of repute, a man of flesh and
blood, was hard to resist in such an uncertain landscape. I
knew that by identifying Zichmni as Henry Sinclair I was
bound to interpret the narrative and the Zen map in a certain
way—and that it might not always be the most accurate one.
Still, I took my chances and pressed on with my quest.

If Zichmni was Henry Sinclair, I asked myself, where
would he have sailed after his campaign in the Faroes? The
likeliest answer is that he would have sailed back to Orkney,
his home base. I checked the map of Frislanda and noticed
that several place-names on the eastern coast had indeed a
greater affinity with place-names in Orkney than with place-
names in the Faroes. Offais, for example, brought to my
mind today's town of Orphir; Dui seemed a misspelling of
the island of Hoy; Rodea evoked Ronaldsay; the island of
Strome, long thought to be the island of Streymoy, in the
Faroes, by Zen aficionados, now seemed to me more likely
to be the small island of Stroma, in the Pentland Firth. Thus,
while the names on the western coast of Frislanda seemed
traceable to the Faroes, those on the eastern coast seemed
to belong to Orkney. In the end I wondered whether Frislanda was not so much a clumsy misrepresentation of the
Faroes as an even clumsier one of the Faroes *and* Orkney
combined.

Clearly I was disassembling Nicolò the Younger's map to
suit my own conjecture. But if Frislanda was indeed a combination of the Faroes and Orkney, it followed that when
Zichmni set sail to "the city of Frislanda," he was not headed

to Tórshavn (which anyway did not exist except as an old
meeting place of tribal chiefs during the earlier Viking days)
but to Kirkwall, the main city in Orkney and the largest
commercial harbor in the region.*

SO THE fog lifted, as it were, and I saw in my mind's eye the
small fleet with the returning soldiers and their Venetian
companions make its way into the bay, past the fishing boats
and the cargo ships laden with stockfish. As they drew closer
to shore, the great church of Saint Olaf came into view,
standing proudly on the waterfront. The boats pulled right
up to the steps in front of the church and the seamen took
down the sails and unloaded their war booty to the sound of
festive cheers. I imagined them filing into Saint Olaf to
attend a Te Deum, the Venetians surely impressed by the
finely carved crosses and the gold and silver calices and reliquaries. As customary, the soldiers' return was celebrated
with a boisterous victory banquet in a smoke-filled hall rich
with the smell of roasted meats and ale.

The town would still have had the vague appearance of an
old Viking settlement. The waterfront, overlooking a wide
firth, bustled with seamen, merchants and craftsmen. The
main street ran parallel to it and was lined with gabled long-
houses, most of which had a shop in the front and sleeping
quarters in the back and a yard where hens and pigs scurried
about. In the best houses the living quarters had wood panel-
ing and tapestries on the walls and good, sturdy furniture.

* Like so many others before me, I puzzled over the fact that Nicolò
the Younger did not draw the Orkney archipelago on his map. After all,
even the Romans were familiar with the Orcades, as they were known in
Latin, and the islands certainly appeared on most Renaissance maps of
the North Atlantic. After a closer look at the Zen map, however, I realized that in fact he *had* drawn the Orkney Islands, albeit a simplified,
miniaturized version of them, which he set (correctly) between Scotland and Frislanda. He did not call them the Orcades, as Renaissance
mapmakers generally referred to them, but Podanda—clearly a misspelling of Porlanda.

At the time, the earl of Orkney did not have a castle or a palace of his own—a fortress and a palace were constructed later. The largest building in Kirkwall, not counting the Church of Saint Olaf, was the Bishop's Palace, a dark red sandstone structure built on a hill overlooking the town. Its last occupant was Bishop William, an avowed enemy of Henry Sinclair who had connived with the Scots to wrest control of Orkney from the king of Norway. Bishop William had been murdered in 1382, the year before Messer Nicolò's arrival, and it was said that the earl of Orkney himself had had a hand in his death.

There were many parts of Henry Sinclair's life that would remain obscure to me, including his role in the bishop's murder. But fortunately there were also facts and figures and historical records that I could rely on to reconstruct his life—as well as a fascinating document that shed light on his role in the complicated relations between Norway and Scotland in the fourteenth century.

Henry Sinclair

HENRY'S FATHER, William Sinclair, was a member of the minor Scottish nobility and a protégé of the powerful Ross clan. His mother, Isabella, was the second daughter of Malise Sperra, earl of Orkney and a vassal of the Norwegian Crown. This mixed heritage played an important role in shaping Henry's life at a time—the second half of the fourteenth century—when Scottish influence in the North Sea was growing at the expense of the old Norse kingdom.

At Rosslyn Castle, a beautiful spot in the Esk Valley, just south of Edinburgh, Henry received what was then a typical upbringing for a young Scottish nobleman. He was taught Latin, French and romance poetry. He learned to ride, to use a bow, to handle a spear and to fight with a sword—they say his favorite game was to pretend he was fighting the English at the battles of Roslin Moor and Bannockburn.

When he was thirteen, his father died in Prussia fighting on the side of the Teutonic knights against the Turks (in this, Henry and Messer Nicolò were alike, both losing their fathers to the Turks when they were very young). Hard times followed for the Sinclairs of Rosslyn, and it was only thanks to Henry's mother, Isabella, and her claim to the Earldom of Orkney, that the family fortunes were eventually reversed.

Long the crown jewel of the Norse kingdom, the Earldom of Orkney was at the center of a power struggle between rising Scotland and declining Norway. Earl Malise Sperra, Henry's grandfather on his mother's side, died around 1350. He had one daughter, Matilda, from his first marriage, and four from his second marriage, among whom was Henry's mother, Isabella. He willed the earldom to Isabella, his favorite, rather than to Matilda, the eldest. But King Haakon VI of Norway had the last word, and he vetoed Malise's transmission of the title because he wanted to choose the new earl himself to make sure the ties of Orkney to the mother country did not loosen any further and the earldom didn't fall under Scottish influence.

In the belief that a Scandinavian would prove more reliable than a Scot, King Haakon entrusted the earldom to Erengisle Suneson, the Swedish husband of Henry's aunt Agneta. But Suneson turned out to be a scheming, unreliable governor and was soon dismissed. For several years, the king sent ineffectual Norwegian emissaries to collect taxes and handle properties. The Crown's authority steadily declined as the power-hungry bishop of Orkney, William IV, increased his hold on the islands and made life impossible for the king's envoys.

Young Henry, encouraged by his mother, began to cultivate his Norse heritage with a keen eye on the earldom. In 1362, at the age of eighteen, he sailed to Copenhagen to attend the wedding of King Haakon. The bride was the daughter of King Waldemar of Denmark, ten-year-old Margaret, who would grow up to rule all of Scandinavia. King

Haakon was gracious to Henry, even recognizing the validity of his mother's claim to Orkney. Still, he refused to bestow the title on her.

Henry got on with his life. He married Janet, the daughter of wealthy Lord Halyburton of Dirleton Castle, who lived twenty miles from Rosslyn Castle. They had at least six children: three boys and three girls. The marriage strengthened Henry's position within the Scottish nobility and increased the family landholdings in Scotland, but his attention remained fixed on the Earldom of Orkney.

In 1375 King Haakon appointed Henry's cousin Alexander de Ard, son of Earl Malise's first daughter, Matilda, as his representative in Orkney. The term was only for a year: the king wanted to test his ability to rein in the unruly Bishop William and manage the collection of taxes more efficiently. But Alexander was not up to the task and the appointment was not renewed.

Henry finally stepped into the breach, skillfully negotiating not just a limited appointment but the title to the earldom itself. The contract is one of few documents from that period to have survived and provides a useful window on the politics of the region at the time.

Henry's primary responsibility was to ensure the collection of taxes on the Crown's properties. In exchange, he was allowed to keep the revenue from the fines he levied for missed or late payments. His main income, of course, would come from the taxes raised on the earl's personal properties. Orkney being the richest land in the Norse realm, Henry stood to make a fortune.

The title, however, came with a long list of obligations. Henry was to protect the islanders and defend Orkney. He could not break the king's peace by going off to war, but if the king requested his help outside the earldom, he would have to serve him with "up to a hundred armed men."

The contract made it clear that he was holding the islands in trust. He could not sell them or even pledge them to obtain loans, he was to receive the king and his followers

with great hospitality, and he was not allowed to build fortifications because they could be used to keep the Crown's
forces from landing in Orkney.

It followed that Henry's heirs would not automatically
inherit the earldom and that he himself would lose the title if
he was found in breach of his oath of fealty. Still, it was a
notable coup on Henry's part because it suddenly elevated
him to a position of considerable influence in the region.

The king had evidently concluded that Henry would be
more effective than either his uncle Erengisle Suneson or his
cousin Alexander de Ard. But that alone would not have
done the trick: in the end, Henry had to agree to deposit
"one thousand golden pieces of English money" into the
coffers of cash-strapped King Haakon the following year
before the Feast of Saint Martin.

Henry sailed to Norway in the summer of 1379. An elaborate ceremony was held in the town of Marstrand, near
Göteborg, attended by the royal family, the court dignitaries
and Church officials. He rendered his oath of fealty to the
king, kissed his hands and then kissed him on the mouth, as
was the custom. King Haakon, in turn, inducted him into the
royal council and bestowed upon him the title of earl of
Orkney, a position of the highest rank in the Norwegian
Kingdom, immediately following the royal princes and the
archbishop of Trondheim.

Yet behind all the pomp and majesty, King Haakon
remained suspicious. It was not enough that a number of
Scottish noblemen serve as guarantors for Henry by provid-
ing sureties in the form of open letters attached to the official
document of investiture. The king insisted that four members of the delegation remain in Norway as hostages until
payment of the thousand golden pieces was received. Among
the four was Malise Sperra, Henry's first cousin and himself
a claimant to the earldom. The king was so worried that the
troublemaking Malise might challenge the document that he
made him sign a specific clause of renunciation. It was
Henry's responsibility to make sure Malise did not violate it.

The following year, before the Feast of Saint Martin, Henry paid the sum he had pledged—it is not clear whether he borrowed it against his future revenues in Orkney or whether he raised the money in Scotland. The hostages, including Malise, were allowed to leave Norway. But before the year was over, King Haakon was dead. His son Olaf was only five years old, so his Danish mother, Queen Margaret, took over the reins of government, opening the way for a Danish takeover of the Norwegian Kingdom.

Queen Margaret needed to reestablish control over the Faroes in order to collect revenues from the rebellious population. But her kingdom had fallen on such hard times that she probably did not have the means to launch a military expedition. Besides, she was so embroiled in the struggle at home to preserve the crown for her young son that she could ill afford to devote herself to her dominions at sea. If Zichmni was indeed Henry Sinclair, then the most plausible explanation for his presence in the Faroes at the time of Messer Nicolò's landing is that Queen Margaret, taking advantage of the earl of Orkney's obligation to the Crown, ordered him to sail north with "up to a hundred armed men"—as the title stated—to take control of the islands. And once he had completed his mission, he made his way back to his earldom.

A Turn in Orkney

DURING A STOPOVER in London on my way to the Orkney Islands, I took a train down to Haslemere, an hour south of the city, in Surrey, to pay a courtesy visit to Niven Sinclair. Although not a direct descendant of Henry Sinclair, he was his most energetic and vocal apologist.

Niven met me at the station. I knew him to be well into his eighties but his jovial disposition made him seem younger than his age. Over lunch at the local Italian restaurant, he told me about his days as a cashew farmer in Tanzania after

World War II. He had lost his farm when the country had become independent and had been repatriated. "I arrived in London with nothing but the bush clothes I had on," he said, digging into his veal scaloppine. His entrepreneurial drive did not desert him. He found a job driving a cab and soon took over the company. Within a few years he was running one of London's top car services and making a small fortune in the process.

Retired and childless, Niven was now free to devote himself and much of his money to his passion for Henry Sinclair. Which meant that he was often up at Rosslyn Castle, in Scotland. It was Henry's grandson, William Sinclair, who later built Rosslyn Chapel, which became famous all over the world after the publication of Dan Brown's *The Da Vinci Code*. Niven helped restore the chapel and preserve the ruins of the castle and was now busy making a permanent arrangement for the Sinclair papers and library.

After lunch, we drove to his home, a rambling stone house overlooking a terraced garden filled with roses and irises and rhododendron. "Henry, you see, was no small Scottish laird," he said as he walked me around the grounds. "He was a visionary leader who had in mind a vast commonwealth stretching all the way to North America to counter the power of the Hanseatic League."

Niven was convinced that Henry had sailed to North America with Messer Nicolò's brother, Antonio, and had established a colony in New England a century before Christopher Columbus crossed the Atlantic. This particular story was very popular among Henry Sinclair devotees on both sides of the Atlantic. But it seemed just as far-fetched to me as it had when I had first heard it from the American tourist who had wandered into the public library in Venice. For the time being, I was more interested in Henry's role in Norse-Scottish relations at the end of the fourteenth century. So I was grateful when Niven brought out books and letters and articles he had collected over the years and proceeded to pile them up on my outstretched arms.

"I can't carry any more," I warned after a while, teetering under the weight of all that paper.

"Yes you can," Niven insisted, producing yet another set of biographical notes. He added melodramatically, "Believe me, from now on you'll need all the ammunition you can take."

A few days later, I flew to Aberdeen and took a ferry to Kirkwall.

Unlike the Faroes, tall and sharp-edged, the Orkney Islands are low-lying and locked in an easy embrace devised by Nature to protect them from rough seas, beating gales and perennial rains. A great number of firths, sounds, bays and "gulfs" (to use Nicolò the Younger's word) fill the Orkney perimeter. The largest of these is Scapa Flow, a calm inner sea that serves as a center of gravity for this family of old islands.

The first migrants arrived in the Orkney Islands during the Neolithic Age and the remains of their primitive round houses are still scattered in the open landscape: stately stones standing firmly in the moors like ageless Giacometti statues. When the Pictish tribes reached these shores, fleeing north-bound Roman legions, they took over the crumbling round houses that survived from prehistoric times and turned them into fortified brochs that towered over the surrounding villages. The Picts were peaceful people who farmed and tended to their animals; they did not brave the high seas and only fished close to shore. Gospel-carrying missionaries converted them to Christianity as early as the seventh century, turning these islands into the northernmost outpost of medieval Europe. In the following century the Picts bore the brunt of the first Viking raids. Each spring, mighty warrior ships carried by strong westerly winds brought terror and destruction to these tranquil islands.

One's heart goes out to the unlucky Picts, who fled from

a mighty enemy coming from the south only to be destroyed by another mighty enemy coming from the north.

In due time the Vikings too settled down to farm and trade. The Orkney Islands flourished and Kirkwall became one of the great commercial centers of the Norwegian realm.

THE LAYOUT and size of Kirkwall ("Church Bay" in the old Viking language) have not changed much since medieval times except that the sea has receded and what used to be the waterfront is now well within the town. The old Romanesque church of Saint Olaf that looked out on the bay in medieval times no longer exists but for an original stone portal that was fitted into the new cathedral built in the nineteenth century and dedicated to Saint Magnus.

The ferry terminal has been moved a few miles out of town so there are only small fishing boats puttering about in the harbor. I was told that until not so long ago the last remnants of the once formidable Kirkwall fortress still stuck out of the water. Some say that Henry Sinclair himself built the castle in the shallow waters of the harbor after he became the earl of Orkney. But it seems unlikely that he would have violated his oath of loyalty to the Crown in such a blatant fashion. Besides, official documents state that his service was nothing but faithful. The illegal castle was probably built by his son, Henry II. And when Henry Sinclair's grandson, William, became the earl in 1434, he was ordered by the Crown to destroy the fort because it had been built without royal consent. But it wasn't torn down until two centuries later. By then the Orkney Islands had passed under the control of the Scottish Crown. When the English laid siege to the harbor they had such a difficult time blasting the castle they claimed it was built by the devil himself. After its demolition, the crumbling pile of rocks in the middle of the harbor served as a reminder of English determination to quash Scottish resistance. Weather and seawater erosion finally had the better of those stones, and today there is no visible trace of the Sinclair fortress.

The ruins of the old Bishop's Palace, on the other hand, are still there on the hillside behind the main street. They retain a certain gloomy grandeur. Crows build their nests in them and swoop in and out of the crumbling walls letting out their sinister croaks.

In town, they say that Bishop William's restless ghost still haunts those old stones.*

King Haakon had been unhappy with Bishop William for a long time. The bishop had taken advantage of the weakened presence of the Norwegian Crown to extend his power in Orkney by ruthlessly enforcing the payment of tithes and Peter's Pence on impoverished islanders and confiscating the property of those who could not pay in order to increase his landholdings. The problem had been exacerbated by the Great Schism of 1378, which had split the Church in two and produced a pope in Rome, Urban VI, and one in Avignon, Clement VII. Norway had sided with the Roman pope whereas Scotland had come down on the side of the Avignon pope. Bishop William was backed by Clement VII and by Scotland, so Norway considered him not just a scoundrel and a thief but a usurper as well.

When Henry Sinclair took over the earldom he found himself in a difficult position. As a Scotsman he was expected to side with Bishop William. But as a vassal of the Norwegian Crown he had to oppose him. Indeed King Haakon had made it plain to Henry, in entrusting the earldom to him, that he was counting on him to neutralize the threat posed by Bishop William to the Crown's authority in

---

* I learned that the ghost of Bishop William shared the premises with another, older and more famous ghost. The great King Haakon IV, returning home aboard his flagship *Krossuden* after his defeat in the Hebrides (with the Treaty of Perth of 1266 Norway renounced all claims on the Isle of Man and the Hebrides while Scotland agreed that Orkney and Shetland would remain a part of Norway), stopped in Orkney, fell ill and died in the Bishop's Palace.

Orkney. Tensions continued to build between Henry and William until 1382, when the bishop was slain. Was Henry responsible for his death? So much time has gone by that it is impossible to say so with certainty. But it was clearly to King Haakon's advantage not to have William around anymore, and if there was foul play it is hard to imagine that Henry did not have a hand in it. In any event, the Avignon pope and the Rome pope both named successors, but neither took office and the see remained vacant for several years.

I RENTED a bicycle one day and rode out to the island of Burray to pay a visit to Willie Thomson, Orkney's local historian. He was something of an institution on the islands. Then retired, he had been for a long time the popular headmaster of Papdale Primary School, in Kirkwall, and for an even longer time before that, a history teacher in Orkney and Shetland.

It was one of those beautiful clear days after a period of wind and rain. Along the way I made the mistake of stopping by the Highland Park distillery to see how Orkney whiskey was distilled. I was running a little ahead of schedule so my idea was to have a quick look around the malting house, the peat-fired kiln and the vats of mash and wash and quickly get back on the road. An hour later, I staggered out of the distillery and struggled to get back on my bicycle. "You will find it is good fuel for the road," I heard the manager chuckle as he waved me off.

Burray was no more than twelve miles away but I felt wobbly in my seat. The breeze was blowing against me and the road went up and down an endless series of green hills. I reached my destination exhausted and late for my appointment.

Thomson was waiting for me in a glassed-in porch that looked out on the bay. Mrs. Thomson brought out a jug of fresh water, some coffee and a plate of butter pancakes served with delicious Orkney cheese, and sat with us to chat.

Within minutes the sky grew dark and the rain swept in from the sea.

Thomson answered my questions about Orkney history with the patience accumulated in a lifetime of teaching. He had words of praise for Henry Sinclair and said he took his duties as the earl of Orkney very seriously. "However, he didn't live here permanently. In winter, he returned to Rosslyn Castle to look after his affairs in Scotland and spend time with his family. He had very good connections in Norway and was frequently in Scandinavia to attend to his duties, but he was mostly concerned with his Scottish estates. He was a Lothian gentleman after all."

My host could not have been more amiable. But when I brought up the topic of the Zen voyages he demurred. In the town library in Kirkwall I had noticed that Thomson had dealt very sympathetically with the Zen story in the first edition of his *History of Orkney* but had expunged his comments in the latest edition. I asked him about this. He told me that Brian Smith, a former pupil of his at Lerwick Grammar School and now the chief archivist at the library in Lerwick, Shetland, had persuaded him that the story of the Zen voyages was a fictitious account.

"And what about Zichmni?" I asked.

"Smith says he was probably just a pirate," Thomson said as he leaned over the table to offer me a pancake with a slice of cheese.

Clearly, it was with Brian Smith in mind that Niven had loaded me with "ammunition" at our meeting in Haslemere. For Smith, I would soon discover, was the driving force behind the anti-Zen front in the region. In an article published in *The New Orkney Antiquarian Journal* he once described the Zen voyages as "tripe" and elevated Nicolò the Younger to the rank of "most blatant hoaxer in the history of the art." But I suspected that what rankled Niven the most was Smith's habit of dismissing Henry Sinclair as a laird of "middling rank."

We said good-bye on the porch and I promised Thomson

I would call on his former pupil when I reached Shetland. "He was a brilliant student," he insisted. "One of my very best."

THE SKY had cleared and I rode back along the eastern shore of Scapa Flow and across the Churchill Barriers to East Mainland. During World War II, the British navy hid much of its fleet in this sheltered inner sea, which used to have four natural openings. For reasons of defense, two of those openings on the eastern shore had been blocked out with stone barriers erected by Italian prisoners of war encamped on Lamb Holm, a small, windswept island between Burray and East Mainland.

The Italian prisoners were quite popular on the island. They set up a music band and a *teatro italiano*. They were for the most part artisans, masons, *contadini*, and they loved to make things with their hands. They built a small church by soldering two Nissen huts, plastering the interior and embellishing the building with a stucco portal. The young master builder, Daniele Chiocchetti, painted religious scenes on the walls.

The old campsite on Lamb Holm had long since reverted to green pastures and was dotted with fluffy sheep when I passed by. The little church was still there, though, and seemed in surprisingly good condition. I was told that Chiocchetti had returned not so long before on a nostalgic visit and had retouched the frescoes.

Despite the breeze and the strong smell of the grass and the sea, it was enough to step inside the little building to recognize the sweet, dank odor of Catholic sacristies all over the world.

BY THE time Messer Nicolò arrived in the region, a year after Bishop William's death, Henry Sinclair had consolidated his hold on the earldom, settling important land disputes and reorganizing a complex tax system. Agriculture had collapsed in the wake of the Great Plague (1349–50), but Henry had encouraged the reoccupation of the land, which had lain fallow during a generation for lack of farmhands. However, if the Orkney economy was growing it was largely because the islands were fast becoming an important link in the booming European fish trade.

Scapa Flow was at the center of this transformation. Every day fishermen hauled tons of cod onto the beach, where an army of workmen busied themselves splitting, boning, filleting and hanging each fish to dry on wooden racks that were laid out in double and triple rows along the beach. Cod was king, of course, but the daily catch might include haddock, mackerel, ling, herring, coalfish and whiting. Foreign merchant ships arrived in increasing numbers to load up, mostly on stockfish (wind-dried cod) destined for the great markets of northern Europe. Fish-processing plants along the shore also guaranteed a steady supply of cod liver oil—another staple of medieval trade in the northern countries (it was used as a lubricant on the rolling logs over which ships were transported on land, in addition to being a part of the traditional Norse diet).

Impressed by the commercial possibilities that seemed to open up in the region, Messer Nicolò wrote to his brother Antonio in Venice, sometime in late 1383, urging him to join him. "Many ships come here to take large consignments of fish and head back to Flanders, Brittany, England, Scotland, Norway and Denmark," he reported, adding as an enticement that "great fortunes are amassed here in this way." Presumably, Antonio did not receive the letter until the following year at the earliest, that is in the summer of 1384. "He purchased a ship in Venice," the narrative said, "and headed out to join his brother, for he was just as eager as Messer Nicolò to see the world, experience life with different peoples and achieve some measure of greatness in this way."

Setting up an expedition to the North Sea was not as simple a task as Nicolò the Younger implied. Antonio must have reached the Orkney Islands no earlier than the summer of 1385. Messer Nicolò "greeted him with great joy because he was his brother, and a very worthy one." But they were soon separated again because Zichmni ordered Messer Nicolò to join him in a new military expedition in the north.

This was another instance in which the lives of Zichmni and Sinclair seemed to match.

Estlanda

ALTHOUGH HENRY SINCLAIR had established his power in the Earldom of Orkney, his authority did not go unchallenged for very long. His cousin and rival, Malise, who now called himself Lord Skaldale, had settled in the town of Orphir, a few miles south of Kirkwall, toward the island of Hoy, after his release as a hostage in Norway. Tensions ran high between the two cousins and conflict finally broke out when Malise made a surprise land grab in Shetland. Claiming a right to rule the islands as a direct descendant of a Shetland folk hero, Ivan Sperra, he took over the huge estates of the Hafthorsson brothers, absentee land-lords who belonged to a wealthy Scandinavian family, and placed his own agents to run the farms. The Crown was too weak to fight back on its own but it had the authority to summon Henry to action in defense of its dominion. The earl of Orkney's oath of allegiance was clear: "If any may wish to attack or hostilely invade the land of Hjalt-land [Shetland], we promise and oblige to defend the lands named."

History books did not say how Henry responded to this act of open hostility by his cousin. But I thought this was a case in which the Zen narrative fit well with the record and could actually help to fill in the blanks. Nicolò the Younger wrote that Zichmni made Messer Nicolò a commandant of his fleet and they sailed north "in full military regalia" to

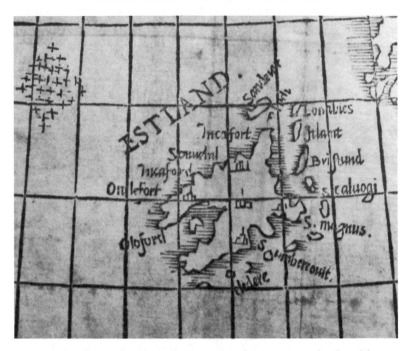

*Estlanda (Estland on the map) is almost certainly the old
Norse dominion of Hjaltland (Shetland). However, Nicolò
Zen the Younger seems to have removed most of the
islands surrounding Mainland.*

take control of Shetland. According to my reading of the
Zen narrative, the Shetland campaign started in the spring of
1384 or 1385 at the latest—roughly the time of Malise's
takeover of the Hafthorsson estates.

With a good wind, it was possible to sail in just one day
from North Ronaldsay, the northernmost Orkney island, to
Sumburgh Head, on the southern tip of Mainland, the
largest of the Shetland Islands. But the crossing was often
rough, especially between Fair Isle and Sumburgh Head,
where the Atlantic Drift collided with the North Sea current,
creating the turbulent tide-race the Vikings called the *roost*.
It was a terrifying sight, that endless line of sea mountains
crashing furiously against one another. The waves seemed to
beat on an invisible reef barrier in the open sea. But unless an

inexperienced seaman got trapped in the *roost,* the danger was largely illusory. The Vikings knew how to sail in it. The Picts, on the other hand, were so afraid of the *roost* they never fished offshore. I was told that when the Vikings first raided Shetland they used to take the trembling Picts out into the *roost* just for laughs.

The storm that hit Zichmni's fleet during the passage to Shetland, on the other hand, was real enough. Several vessels were lost and the remaining ships were wrecked on an island called Grislanda. My guess is that Grislanda was Fair Isle, the only substantial island between Orkney and Shetland, known for its shipwrecks and its wide-open heather moors (*grisla*). But Nicolò the Younger made a notable blunder: he confused Eslanda/Estlanda (Shetland) with Islanda (Iceland). He therefore breezily placed Grislanda below Iceland on his map rather than below Shetland. As a result, his narrative became terribly twisted. For example, he wrote that once Zichmni, Messer Nicolò and the rest of the survivors had repaired their few remaining ships in Grislanda, they continued their journey, not to nearby Shetland (Estlanda), where they were actually headed and where Malise was waiting for them, but to Iceland (Islanda)!

MY OWN passage from Kirkwall to Lerwick on the overnight ferry was smooth—the *roost* no more than a low rumble against the heavy iron keel of the ferry. In the bar lounge, two fiddlers, an accordion player and a guitarist on their way to a folk festival sang Celtic ballads through the night. At dawn we passed Sumburgh Head and arrived in Lerwick, a town of grey buildings and surprisingly wide avenues built in the days of the kelp boom of the late nineteenth century.

It was a beautiful, clear day and the wet pastures of Shetland glistened in the early morning sun. I observed the coastline with Zichmni's beleaguered fleet in mind. The great slabs of reddish sandstone seemed hardly impregnable. Open coves and wide sandy beaches would have made for an easy landing. But Zichmni's men were "few and poorly armed" after the shipwreck. The assault was repelled and they gave up the plan to take Mainland, the largest island of the Shetlands, choosing instead to raid some of the smaller ones of the archipelago. Nicolò the Younger mentioned seven: Talas, Broas, Iscant, Trans, Mimant, Damberc and Bres. The last two were easily identifiable: Damberc comes from Danaberg, a sound near Lerwick, and Bres was clearly the island of Bressay. The others were more difficult to identify, but their number was roughly equivalent to the islands facing the eastern coast of Mainland (Unst, Yell, Fetlar, Whalsay, the Out Skerries, Mousa, Bressay).

Of course Nicolò the Younger was still operating on the assumption that the campaign was taking place in Iceland rather than Shetland. In drawing the Zen map he bunched up those seven islands and placed them next to Islanda rather than Estland, only adding to the confusion.

I ARRANGED to meet Smith at his office in the archives building in Lerwick, a glass and steel structure set in a nineteenth-century cityscape. I suspected he would not be thrilled to see me but I wasn't quite ready for the cold reception in the hall. He came toward me stiff and unsmiling, pushing back the long black bangs that framed his boyish face.

He led me to his office at a brisk pace by way of a back staircase. "I hear you are skeptical about the Zen voyages," I blithely said to break the ice as we climbed the stairs. Smith turned to me and I thought for a moment he was going to pin me to the wall. "I am certainly *not* a skeptic," he hissed. "I believe the story is pure rubbish." In his office I made several useless efforts to revive the conversation. He had no interest in exploring the possibilities the Zen story offered and seemed entirely immune to that special Zen vibration that had carried me all the way from Venice to the cramped office I was sitting in. Clearly he was irritated by my presence.

"You have been sent by Niven, haven't you?" Smith suddenly asked. I told him that I had indeed met Niven but assured him I was not his secret agent and was paying for my own expenses. "There is no point in arguing," Smith answered curtly. "My job after all is to help people find the books they are looking for."

With that, he got up and led me to the reading room. And true to his word, he transformed himself into the most obliging librarian. "I hope these will be useful," he said, handing over a pile of documents on local history. "I look forward to reviewing your book," he said with a grin, and with that he disappeared.

THE NARRATIVE said that at the end of the summer, following his unsuccessful campaign in Estlanda, Zichmni returned to Frislanda with "what remained of his army." Messer Nicolò did not go with him for he wanted to sail north to Iceland the following spring. Before leaving, Zichmni gave orders to build a fort on Bressay, presumably to protect the few ships he was leaving behind with Messer Nicolò.

I had brought with me to Lerwick a snapshot of a pile of reddish sandstones in shallow waters that Niven had taken several years before and had given to me when I had gone to see him.

"Here is the Fort of Bressay," he had told me with great assurance.

I took the ferry across to Bressay to look for Niven's pile of stones. The island, no more than ten square miles, was dominated by Ward Hill, one of the highest points in Shetland (742 feet). Vikings used to send smoke signals from the summit; on a clear day, one can see the entire archipelago from its summit. I found no villages on the island, only a few scattered farms. Long-abandoned croft houses stood in the meadows like tired old ghosts. Sheep grazed in the pastures that sloped to the sea. Swooping curlews and arctic skimmers peeped and sang to their heart's content. At low tide, large families of seals came to lie on the wet sand to enjoy the sun.

In medieval times, a low-lying promontory known as Leira Ness stretched out into Bressay Sound forming a natural haven from western gales; it was the only place on the island where vessels could easily be beached or anchored for the winter. Over the centuries the rising sea submerged the promontory. Only the southern tip remained above water: the holm of Leira Ness, with its tumble of sandstones wreathed by strands of soggy kelp. Niven was sure those stones were the remains of the Fort of Bressay.

ON THE edge of the water, facing the holm of Leira Ness, was an old whitewashed farmhouse with three chimneys. Jonathan Wills, a marine biologist and nature guide, lived there with his family. I knocked on the door and introduced myself as a friend of Niven's. Jonathan and his wife, Leslie, welcomed me with a glass of red wine and kindly added a plate at the table.

After dinner, glass still in hand, Jonathan walked me over to the holm, which could be reached in waders at low tide. Leira Ness looked indeed like the perfect place to build a fort for the commanding view it afforded of Bressay Sound. But Jonathan chafed at the idea, adding that Niven, whom he had met on several occasions to discuss the Fort of Bressay, got easily carried away. "If ever a fort was built on Bressay it would have been in this bay," he conceded. "But there is no archaeological evidence there ever was one." I made the rather weak point that the rectangular stones piled on the holm certainly *appeared* to be old ruins. "Bressay sandstone splits naturally into blocks that look like old building material," Jonathan replied impatiently. "The local masons call it 'freestone.' "

We walked back home through his gale-battered vegetable garden. I could see he was far more keen to talk about his epic battle to grow onions, asparagus, potatoes and strawberries in such a difficult climate than about the elusive mystery of the Fort of Bressay. And after a while I saw his point. A light breeze was bringing an aria from Verdi's *Il Trovatore* from the house. The air was rich with the smell of black earth and dried algae. Standing in his onion plot, Jonathan turned to the northern sky, still luminous despite the late hour.

"From here," he said, sweeping the air with his raised glass, "it is a straight line to Iceland."

As he spoke it occurred to me that at these latitudes a traveler from southern Europe ceases to look back with yearning to the Mediterranean because the pull of the Great North becomes irresistible.

Messer Nicolò must have felt a similar attraction; I pictured him settling down for the winter, his thoughts already busy with plans for the following spring.

Life in Shetland hadn't changed much since the days of the Vikings. The last of the peat was cut at the end of the summer and stacked and carried by pony—the famous Shetland ponies!—to the farmsteads. Soon it was time to churn butter and make cheese. Wool was washed, teased and dyed with herbs and mosses. Cod and herring were set out to dry in the wind. The men went seal hunting. Later in the autumn, the grain was milled. Cows that wouldn't survive the winter were slaughtered; their meat was salted, the hides tanned, the bones shaped into tools. During the long winter months there was not much to do except repair boats and mend fishing nets and lines.

By early spring the cycle started anew. The cows that had survived the winter were put to pasture, pigs and hens were let out to roam and barley was planted. In May the fishing season began and the men went out to sea. As for Messer Nicolò, "he rigged up his three ships and sailed north" to explore other lands.

CHAPTER FIVE

Islanda

IT TOOK no less than two weeks to reach Iceland from Shetland following the old Viking route: four or five days of navigation to the Faroes, a brief stop to stock up on supplies before sailing out into the North Atlantic, and then another week of steady sailing on a northwestern course toward the Arctic. Seamen used to say that on a clear day they would catch their first glimpse of the shimmering glaciers — a tiny white speck on the northern horizon — a good one hundred miles before reaching the black shores of Iceland.

The shallow waters of the southern coast were notoriously treacherous. Searching for a safe landfall, Messer Nicolò navigated carefully between sandbars until he sailed into a wide fjord and reached a sheltered bay with a good harbor. Several foreign vessels were anchored there — English and German merchant ships loading their cargoes of fish. The waterfront was busy with seamen, dockhands, traders and craftsmen going about their daily business. And at the center of all that bustle, overlooking the bay, was a large monastery with thick walls and vaults and domed roofs. It turned out the monastery was run by industrious monks who spoke Latin among themselves. All around it were small round farmhouses. Sulfurous springs kept the air and the soil and the seawater warm, and an active volcano loomed in the background, at the end of great lava fields. "The place was a wonder to behold," Messer Nicolò wrote home, unable to conceal his surprise.

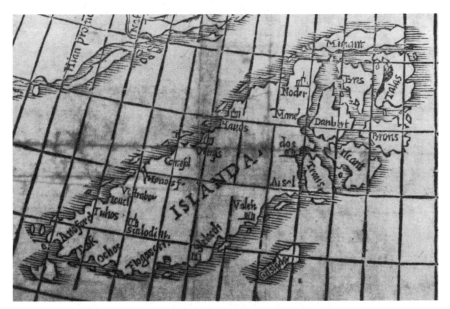

*After spending the winter in Shetland, Messer Nicolò
"rigged up his three ships" and sailed north to Islanda.
Nicolò the Younger drew a set of islands off the eastern
coast of Iceland that appear to belong to Shetland.*

. . .

IN PREHISTORIC times, only birds and fish and a few
species of wild animals lived on this pristine island on the
roof of the world. They say Pytheas of Marseille was the first
European to reach the shores of Iceland while exploring the
Atlantic around 400 BC. He called it Thule—the last island
before the great sea lung of mist and ice and water that
extended beyond the known world. The name Thule lived
on throughout antiquity and was resurrected by cartographers in continental Europe during the Renaissance. But in
northern Europe the island was known by its old Norse
name, Islanda, the Island of Ice.

After Pytheas's foray, no other European came to Iceland
for another thousand years. At the end of the eighth century
a few Irish monks arrived in their sturdy little *currachs*, but

they left few traces of their presence. Thus the official history of Iceland began in 874, the year Ingólfur Arnarson, the first settler, sailed from Norway and built a farmstead near present-day Reykjavik. Other Viking families followed in Ingólfur's wake during the reign of King Harald Finehair. They came from Norway but also Ireland, Shetland and Orkney. During this early period, known as the Age of the Sagas, the settlers established a pagan society run by chieftains who met in their open-air parliament (Althing) in Thingvellir (Pingvellir).

This hallowed valley, still revered today as Iceland's birthplace, is where the American and the European tectonic plates collide to form a choppy, fractured landscape of lichen-covered boulders. A clear stream of glacial water, filled with darting trout, rushes through the rocky divide into a peaceful lake dotted with a hundred grassy islets.

THE EARLY settlers lived in large farming communities scattered around the island and prospered in relative tranquillity. The population grew steadily and by AD 1100 it reached 100,000. But peace broke down in the thirteenth century as tensions between the clans devolved into a spiral of vengeful killings. Norway took advantage of the strife and brought Iceland under its control in 1264. The new colony was forced to trade exclusively through the Norwegian port of Bergen. Every year, six ships sailed from Norway loaded with timber, grains and cloth, which the Icelanders purchased in exchange for dried fish, hides and whalebone.

The Icelandic economy, already suffocating under the effect of these commercial restrictions, was devastated by major volcanic eruptions in 1308, 1321 and 1339. The country was spared the Black Death in midcentury (it came fifty years later). But Norway, already in decline, suffered the plague's full, devastating impact. Terribly weakened, it lost its hold on Iceland. Trade between the two countries dwindled to a trickle, and by the time Messer Nicolò made his voyage to Iceland around 1385 or 1386, not one of the six ships that were supposed to sail every year from Bergen was making the journey anymore. Indeed, the ties between Iceland and the mother country had loosened to the point that, as Messer Nicolò duly noticed upon his arrival, the Crown was no longer able to keep foreign merchants from trading with Icelanders.

MESSER NICOLÒ wrote a long letter home about his stay in Iceland. According to Nicolò the Younger, only a portion of that letter survived—the portion in which he described the monastery and the life the ingenious monks had organized for themselves. Still, his observations were so detailed, his language so precise, that I felt they brought to his nebulous journey a moment of clarity and truth.

What most fascinated Messer Nicolò were the clever ways in which the monks used the hot springs to keep the monastery warm at all times. "For example, scalding water is brought to the rooms of the elders in large containers made of copper, tin or stone," he wrote. "These containers become so hot they are like moveable heating stoves. And somehow," he added with a note of pleasant surprise, "the water does not leave a bad smell in the room."

All around the monastery, the ground was warm enough that the chapel and the cells stayed well heated through the winter, "and if it gets too hot, they simply let in the cold by opening the window."

The cloistered garden was in full bloom during the summer. But plants grew in the winter as well because the air was kept moist thanks to a small aqueduct that brought hot water to a large copper container placed in the center of the cloister. The monks grew vegetables and fruits and herbs during much of the year in their winterized patches. "For this reason, too, the local inhabitants hold them in great awe and bring poultry and meats and other gifts to the monastery."

The monks were able to cook without lighting a fire. They baked bread by simply placing the dough in a copper pan and sliding it in a cooking hole. "The dough rises just like it does in one of our wood-burning ovens," Messer Nicolò noted in amazement.

He was also fascinated by the building materials that were used in the region and the quality of the masonry: "The men go up to the crater of the nearby volcano and extract the red-hot rocks expelled directly from the mouth of the mountain and pour ice-cold water over them. The burning stones crack open, yielding a molten substance similar to lime-based mortar which, once dry, turns into a white powder that can be stored because it never spoils. When the rocks taken from the crater have cooled they are transported down to the monastery and used as building blocks. They are hard but also very light and therefore ideal for construction work. The effect is one of beauty and solidity."

I am sure Nicolò the Younger, an accomplished engineer, appreciated this description of materials and building techniques.

The small round farmhouses near the monastery were only about twenty-five feet in diameter. "The builders start with the external walls," Messer Nicolò explained, "and once they reach the desired height they work their way toward the center, leaving an opening in the middle for light and ventilation. The ground is so warm there is no need to light a fire to heat up the house, so the problem of smoke does not exist."

According to Messer Nicolò, the fjord in front of the monastery never froze because of the geothermal conditions in the area. The fishermen did not have far to go for their daily catch because the waters teemed with trout and salmon. There was also a great abundance of geese, ducks and swans. The monks exchanged goods with the local farmers; they employed them in construction work, of course, but also for the collection of firewood, the gathering of bird's eggs and "a thousand other chores" that came up every day in this thriving, industrious community.

The monastery was well known to foreign traders. Merchants from England and the Hanseatic League, taking advantage of the declining presence of the Norwegians, sailed up the fjord and often spent the winter there. It was an opportunity for them to fix their boats, stock up on provisions and sell timber, grains and cloth to the monks in exchange for dried cod and sealskins.

Messer Nicolò's writing style was factual, informative. I noticed that he never emphasized the exotic element in an attempt to impress readers back home, as later writers of the Renaissance often did, including Nicolò the Younger. Nor did he use a superior tone. He was interested above all in how things worked around him and how they could be turned to advantage. In this he remained the quintessential medieval merchant-traveler, always looking for opportunities even as he made his way on very unfamiliar terrain.

WHEN I first read Messer Nicolò's account I was not aware of the important role monasteries played in Icelandic society during the Middle Ages. Iceland was Christianized around the year 1000 under pressure from Norway. But in the early days of Christianity, Icelanders continued to worship their pagan deities—Odin, the god of war; Thor, the god of seafarers and farmers; Freyr, the god of fertility. Priests were mostly freelancers employed by local landowners who built and owned the churches. These priests lived with concubines and fathered children. One notorious nun, Gróa, was both the daughter of a bishop and the mother of a monk. Baptism was supposed to take place in the freezing waters of Thingvellir, but Icelanders couldn't be bothered, preferring to take the sacrament while bathing in the hot springs near their homes.

A bishop was finally appointed in 1055 to the see of Skálholt, and he introduced the tithe and Peter's Pence. A second bishopric was established in Hólar in 1106. But the bishops were weak and Rome was much too far to enforce tax collection. Thus for a long time the Church of Iceland remained in the hands of local chieftains. It was not until the archbishopric of Trondheim was established in Norway in 1152, with jurisdiction over Iceland, the Faroes and Greenland, that the Church became more structured and autonomous.

By the time Messer Nicolò arrived in Iceland, at the end of the fourteenth century, there were as many as seven monasteries and two nunneries scattered across the country. All of them had been founded by Augustine or Benedictine monks during the twelfth century and had provided stability and continuity to religious life even during periods of great strife. They were prosperous communities and important centers of learning, where the monks copied and translated ancient texts and wrote the great Icelandic sagas—epic narratives set during the years of the first settlements.

But which of these monasteries was the one Messer Nicolò visited?

NICOLÒ THE Younger was less than useful in helping me to identify its location. Believing that Messer Nicolò had sailed from Iceland to Greenland rather than from Shetland to Iceland (because of his earlier confusion between Shetland and Iceland), he placed the monastery in Grolandia, north of Engronelant on his map. To signal the spot, he drew a small volcano in full eruption (even though there were no active volcanoes in Greenland) and a monastery, which he named S. Tomas Zenobium. Brian Smith, and many others after him, thought the word "Zenobium" was a pun by Nicolò the Younger, based on his own family name—the forger's signature, as it were. But it is more likely that "Zenobium" was simply the Latin word "Cenobium," meaning "monastery," spelled in the Venetian manner, with a "z" in lieu of a "c." And the monastery was probably dedicated to Saint

Islanda

Olaf rather than Saint Thomas—given Nicolò the Younger's propensity to muddle things it is easy enough to imagine him reading "S.tomas" for "St.olaf" in a faded script.

My attempt to track Messer Nicolò was further frustrated by the realization that all the monasteries in Iceland had long gone to ruin. The demise of monastic culture was very swift once the Protestant Reformation reached Iceland in 1531. The monasteries themselves were ransacked; sand and volcanic ash slowly buried the buildings until there was nothing left to see. Yet Messer Nicolò's clear, evocative words had seized my imagination. And in a strange way, I felt I owed it to him to find the place he had described with such precision—or at least give him my best effort.

To Thikkvabaejarklaustur

IT IS NO LONGER POSSIBLE to travel by ferry from Shetland to Iceland via the Faroes following the route of medieval navigators. Until a few years ago Smyril Line, a Faroese company, operated regular service between Aberdeen and Reykjavik via Orkney, Shetland and the Faroes. But the company has severed the link between Shetland and the Faroes in order to cut costs, and this ancient North Atlantic thoroughfare is now truncated. In order to follow Messer Nicolò on his northbound journey I made my way back to London and took an Iceland Express flight to Reykjavik from Stansted. Two hours later I landed at Keflavik Airport, west of the capital, on a black, volcanic peninsula strewn with jagged rocks of lava.

I had booked a room through the Internet with a family in Reykjavik. Hreinn and Arna lived with their son and daughter in a small two-floor house that was sheathed with corrugated iron, in the Icelandic fashion, and painted scarlet red. It had a name I liked: Áskot, the House of the God. Trees are a rarity in Iceland and I had chosen Áskot among others in part because it was shaded by a grove of tall mountain ash. Two blocks down the road, on the way downtown, was the old Reykjavik cemetery, with its lichen-covered lava tombstones.

The first night I hardly slept. Darkness came and went sometime between two and four a.m. I staggered down to breakfast and found Arna, my landlady, busily spreading out various types of hams and salamis, hard-boiled eggs, fresh bread and strawberry jam.

I showed surprise at her perkiness.

Arna grinned. "In the spring we like to sleep very little." She was a tall, strong woman with dark eyes and jet black hair with bangs. "We live in darkness half of the year. We want to compensate during the other half, so we stay awake and soak up as much light as we can."

The little red house was only a five-minute walk from the National Library and University. The reading rooms were filled with light. Students were preparing for their final examinations. I read all I could find on monasteries in English-language books on Iceland—which was not very much. It was puzzling to learn that so little had been done to uncover the remains of such an important part of Icelandic civilization. At the suggestion of Margrét Hallgrimsdóttir, the director of the National Museum, I walked over to the museum's Archaeology Department, across the lawn from the National Library, and knocked on the door of Steinunn Kristjánsdóttir, one of very few Icelandic archaeologists with fieldwork experience in unearthing the old monasteries—a few years earlier she had started a project at Skriduklaustur (Skiðuklaustur), in eastern Iceland.

Steinunn seemed intrigued by the story of Messer Nicolò's voyage to Iceland. The next day I brought her an English translation I had prepared of Messer Nicolò's description of the monastery. I asked her why so little archaeological work had been done on the sites of old monasteries. "Icelandic scholars can sometimes be very rigid in their way of thinking," she replied. "It has long been assumed that monasteries were little more than farmhouse extensions. Historians have not wanted to challenge this old theory. But I have come to believe that the monastic model in Iceland was similar to the one which prevailed in much of Europe at the time: here too monasteries were highly developed and largely self-sufficient communities. And they were important centers of culture and learning."

Steinunn pulled out a map of Iceland with all the known sites of old monasteries. In each case we considered the distance from the sea, whether there was a volcano nearby and if there were or might have been hot springs. By a simple process of exclusion, we soon fixed our attention on Thikkvabaejarklaustur, a twelfth-century Augustine monastery in the region of Alftaver, east of the Mýrdal sand desert on the southern coast of Iceland, not far from an area of hot springs and within sight of an active volcano, Mount Katla.

"This would have to be it," Steinunn said, pressing her finger on the map. The area was about a four-hour car drive east of Reykjavik. She wished me good luck. "I suspect there is not much to see there anymore," she cautioned. "The monastery was buried a long time ago. But if you are to make any sense of this story, you must go to Alftaver."

THIKKVABAEJARKLAUSTUR (ÞYKKVABÆJARKLAUSTUR), I learned back at the library, was founded in 1168 by Bishop Klaengur Thorstensson of Skálholt. But in both a practical and a spiritual sense the founding father was Thorlak Thorhallsson—Saint Thorlacius. Young Thorlak arrived at the monastery in 1170 as a prior after his studies in France and England and six years of residence at Kirkjubaer (Kirkjubær or, more commonly, Kirkjubæjarklaustur), a nearby nunnery (it was not uncommon to have priors in nunneries). It says in *Thorlak's Saga*, a hagiographical work written after his death, that "he organized the monks' life so beautifully that wise men said they had never beheld such good morals." Nor such good manners: "He forbade monks from wandering or going every which way who had no pressing need to do so, and bade them to be even-tempered, and to keep complete silence when it was obligatory and use good language when speech was allowed . . . monks went to [his] monastery from other monasteries, both natives and foreigners, to behold and learn good habits there, and each reported that nowhere had they seen the equal of the life which Thorlak had established there."

After seven years at Thikkvabaejarklaustur, Thorlak became bishop of Skálholt. Most churches in Iceland were still the personal property of the big landowning families; Thorlak worked hard to bring them under ecclesiastical rule. He was a staunch supporter of the Gregorian reform, fought hard against the spread of simony (selling religious favors such as indulgences) and did his best to enforce the vow of celibacy—a daunting task even in his own household. One day the local deacon, one Jón Loftsson, seduced Bishop Thorlak's sister, Ragnheid, and moved in with her. Not content to have caused the bishop deep displeasure, Loftsson tried to kill him on at least three occasions. Given the atmosphere at home, Bishop Thorlak was lucky to survive until 1193, when he died of natural causes at the age of sixty.

In the decades following the death of Bishop Thorlak, as clan violence tore up the country, the monastery remained a peaceful, industrious enclave. By the middle of the thirteenth century it was one of the most important centers of learning in Iceland. *Njál's Saga* is supposed to have been written at Thikkvabaejarklaustur. Possibly the greatest of the sagas and certainly Icelanders' favorite book, this epic tale takes place at the time of the settlers in southern Iceland, roughly in the same region as the monastery. It tells the story of Beardless Njál, a wise and learned farmer with the gift of foresight, and his close friend Gunnar, a valiant, tragic figure caught in a spiral of vengeful killings.

Some believe *Njál's Saga* was written by Abbott Brandur Jónsson, who was at Thikkvabaejarklaustur from 1247 to 1262. But no one really knows who the author was because the monastery's archives were lost even before the Reformation. Apparently they were stored in the bell tower that rose high above the church. The tower collapsed after a volcanic eruption or an earth tremor. All documents and manuscripts were either destroyed or scattered by powerful winds.

This particular story was recorded by Árni Magnússon, a great Icelandic antiquarian, when he visited the region in the early eighteenth century. It all happened so quickly, he reported, that nothing was salvaged. On that same occasion, the large bell in the tower—the monks called it Augustine's bell—crashed to the ground and broke into pieces. The fragments were transported to Bessastadir (Bessastaðir), the Danish governor's residence near present-day Reykjavik. Seven horses were needed to pull the carts carrying the great fragments of the bell.

When Magnússon visited Thikkvabaejarklaustur looking for traces of the lost monastery, local farmers were still using parts of the old buildings. The sea had receded and the ruins were on a rise surrounded by marshes, and fairly inaccessible. But in 1755, Mount Katla ("The Great Kettle") exploded in a massive eruption and most of what Magnússon had seen was buried under a thick layer of volcanic ash. Winds and natural erosion further erased the remains of the monastery. Eventually the area was slowly repopulated, and in 1873 a small wooden Lutheran church was erected on top of the old cemetery.

Thordur the Elf

I HAD RENTED A CAR to drive out to the grounds of the monastery. When I went downstairs for breakfast, however, I found my landlady, Arna, in full gear and ready to go. "I am coming with you," she announced. "We can take my car if you pay for the gas." I was glad to have the company of a native speaker.

The fog was low when we left the city; a light rain was falling. We drove across the black lava fields of Mosfellsheidi

(Mosfellheiði) and into the mountains, and the clouds lifted just enough to reveal the snow dappled peaks of Heidin Ha (Heiðin Há). The temperature was surprisingly mild. Although southern Iceland lies just below the Arctic Circle, the climate is relatively temperate thanks to the warming effect of the North Atlantic currents. Even in winter the temperatures seldom drop much below freezing. As we drove by a ski station, Arna said there had been so little snow during the winter that the runs had been closed before the end of the season.

The road ran down the mountains toward Hveragerdi (Hveragerði; "Hot Spring Gardens"), a small town at the epicenter of very intense geothermal activity. We passed by several rows of industrial greenhouses lit up by giant lamps. "They are heated by underground gases and hot sulfurous water," Arna said. "Vegetables and flowers grow all year round."

Some greenhouses were filled with ripe tomatoes, eggplants, peppers and even bananas; others with roses and lilies. I mentioned the monks' winterized gardens to Arna and told her about Messer Nicolò's fascination with their ability to bake bread without having to light a fire. She nodded back, showing little surprise.

Before leaving Hveragerdi we stopped for gas. Arna went into the general store and came back with a sliced loaf of rich, dark, sweet-tasting bread baked locally in ovens heated just like they were six centuries earlier at Thikkvabaejar-klaustur. "*Pottbraud*," she said, handing me a slice. "No need to light a fire."

We drove across the black plain of Selfoss and through the towns of Hella and Hvolsvöllur. On both sides of the road, razor-edged blocks of lava were strewn haphazardly on the flats, mixed with spherical boulders and perfect cones. The effect was of a dark, metaphysical landscape. Mount Hekla, Iceland's fiercest volcano, loomed to our left. It was famous all over Europe for its destructive force even in the

Middle Ages. I had seen a small drawing of it on one of the first maps of Iceland, and this intimidating Latin caption: *"Perpetuis damnata ira et nivibus horrendo boatu lapides evomit"* — "Cursed with eternal ire and snow, Hekla vomits rocks with a hideous sound."

We passed quietly by the sleeping beast.

"ON YOUR way to Thikkvabaejarklaustur you should stop in Skógar to talk to Thordur Tomasson," Steinunn had said to me in Reykjavik. "No one knows the history of the southern region like he does."

Skógar is a small community around Skógafoss, the great waterfall where the melted ice of the Mýrdal Glacier comes crashing down at sea level. They say Thrasi, the first settler in Skógar, hid his treasure behind the sheet of water. One day a young farmer managed to get hold of the iron ring that served as a handle and tried to yank the chest out from behind the waterfall. The handle came off and the chest remained where it was—people say it is still there and that on sunny days one can see the gold shimmer in the spray. The iron ring, on the other hand, is on display at the small folk museum in Skógar that Thordur Tomasson founded thirty years ago.

Thordur was standing at the door of the museum as if he had been waiting for me. He looked like an Icelandic elf: a short man, with a crinkly face and tufts of white hair sprouting from his ears and nose. He was close to ninety, I later learned, but a boyish twinkle lit up his eyes. His generous warmth was magnetic. I felt an urge to hug him—only to realize that he had already wrapped himself around my waist and was holding me very firmly in an awkward embrace.

Thordur told me that he first started poking around the site of Thikkvabaejarklaustur as a young archaeologist in the early 1950s. The monastery had long been buried under layers of ash and debris, but in those days parts of the original buildings were still visible. They could be reached by a raised dirt road that crossed the surrounding marshes. Even though there was very little to see, Thordur was impressed by the way the building stones had been cut. "They were a testimony to the extraordinary craftsmanship of the old masons who lived in the area."

Thordur returned to the site thirty years later. "Icelandic farmers have the good habit of calling an archaeologist when they are about to bulldoze an area of buried ruins," he explained. "My friend Hilmar Jón Brynjolfsson used to farm near Thikkvabaejarklaustur. One day he called me to tell me he planned to dig drainage canals near the old cemetery in order to dry the land; he asked me if I wanted to come over and take a look." The bulldozer dug several trenchlike ditches, two feet wide and six feet deep. Thordur was able to identify an outer wall of the monastery and parts of the pavement. The workmen also dug up a slab of basalt about a foot wide. "It was very worn on the surface," Thordur recollected. "It was clearly a door sill which had been placed at the entrance of the monastery. It was probably quarried in the mountains nearby. They must have used a very robust sled to transport it all the way to Thikkvabaejarklaustur. It was a very inspiring stone: I imagined Saint Thorlacius and his fellow monks coming out and crossing themselves on the way to church at the start of a new day."

In the course of several visits, Thordur found many other medieval artifacts stuck in the turf. He kept most of them under a glass casing in his museum at Skógar. Among the objects he showed me were a wooden spoon, a ladle and other kitchen utensils, old nails, a rusty axe, a twelve-inch door hinge, several crosses, pieces of frayed cloth, a comb made of whalebone, a raggedy black lace purse knitted with an inverted stitch. My favorite, however, was a single rather smart-looking suede shoe with a half sole.

Thordur showed me the road to Thikkvabaejarklaustur on the map and gave me a few pointers on how to avoid getting lost in the Mýrdalssandur, the great sand desert one crossed to reach the old site of the monastery. "Once you've seen the grounds make sure you drive over to my old friend Villi," Thordur said. "He has a farm east of there, at Hnausar, by the Elvatn River. He knows all the old stories."

After Skógar, the road followed the lower end of the Mýrdal Glacier. Mount Katla, whose ash buried Thikk-vabaejarklaustur over the centuries, rises at the center of the snowy mass. We drove through the small town of Vik, then crossed the flat Mýrdalssandur, covered with gnarled stones, little pyramids of lava, fanciful sandcastles with turrets and pinnacles. At the end of what looked like a bizarre geological playground we crossed a dry riverbed and entered a turbulent landscape of hardened magma. But that scenery also ended abruptly and we found ourselves driving through green pastures flecked with Icelandic sheep. Thikkvabae-jarklaustur could not be far, I thought; sure enough, in the distance, I saw the stern little Lutheran church, planted firmly on the ground where the ruins of the old monastery lay buried.

Thordur had told me that the walls of the monastery started immediately to the west of the church, but that I would not be able to see them because now the ruins were entirely covered by a thick layer of turf. I poked around and saw a few small fragments of ancient masonry sprouting here and there like mushrooms. Nothing else. I tried to imagine the place as it had once been, with its herbal gardens and vegetable patches, hot water bubbling in the cloister, succulent smells coming from the kitchens, monks rushing to Matins at the sound of Augustine's bell. It turned into a melancholy effort; a mournful silence had settled over the grounds.

I did find the slab of basalt that, according to Thordur, had served as a door sill at the main entrance of the monastery in the time of the monks. The workmen who had dug it out during the drainage project in the eighties had planted it into the ground vertically. Now it stood there like a solitary tombstone.

Farmer Villi

ARNA AND I HAD BEEN on the road since early morning. A chilly wind was blowing down from the Mýrdal Glacier; it was getting late and I was ready to drive back to Reykjavik. Still, Thordur had insisted we call on his old friend Villi Eyjólfsson, the farmer over at Hnausar, so we continued to drive eastward, across the Kutha Fljot, which was once a deep fjord teeming with fish and bird life and was now a vast and muddy drainage field for the waters of the great southern glaciers. On the other side, the uneven terrain was carpeted as far as the eye could see with thick, emerald-colored moss. "We have entered the Green Planet," Arna said in a monotone.

Villi lived in an isolated farm surrounded by rich pastures. I noticed there were no sheep grazing, however; no farm animals, no pickup truck in front of the house. How did Villi get around? The place was so remote. Arna and I pushed the door open and were about to make our way in when a very tall, broad-shouldered man shuffled forward, filling up the entire frame of the door. He had a warm smile. Thordur had told me Villi was in his mideighties, but he seemed younger than his age and he bore an air of distinction despite his baggy jeans and frayed checkered shirt.

Inside, Villi moved about like a trapped giant, feeling his way along the thin walls and the low plywood ceiling so as not to bump his head. He led us by a small kitchen with an old woodstove, a tiny, disordered bedroom, and into a sitting room with peeling wallpaper, a beat-up old couch, two chairs and a stool on which I noticed a dial telephone from long ago.

Villi settled on the couch. He turned out to be a natural storyteller, a true Icelandic bard who knew all the old sagas and all the family stories handed down from generation to generation by the farmers of southern Iceland. I asked him what he knew about Thikkvabaejarklaustur; he reached back into his seemingly inexhaustible memory and retrieved images from centuries ago that were so vivid as to seem drawn from his own life.

"It was a large monastery," he said in his low, raspy voice. "As many as twenty-five monks lived there during its heyday. They came from Norway but also England and France and other parts of northern Europe because it was a great center of learning." I mentioned *Njál's Saga* to Villi, and he spoke about Njál as if he were speaking of a neighbor or a close friend who had met a tragic destiny. "He was a good man, a peaceful man, a great legal mind. But there were great feuds in this region and his enemies torched Bergthorshvol, his house over by the Ranga River. He died a horrible death, and so did his sons."

Indeed they did. It said in the saga that Old Beardless Njál, who had the gift of foresight, was visited by a vision of his death on the eve of the attack at Bergthorshvol. "Strange things are happening to me," he told his family. "I look around the room and imagine that I see both gable walls gone, and the table and food all covered with blood." He was resigned to die. As his enemies set fire to the house, he told his wife, Bergthora, "We will go to our beds and lie down." And to his foreman: "Now you must see how we lie down and how I lay us out, for I don't intend to budge from this spot, no matter how much the smoke and the fire bother me—then you will know where our remains can be found."

I thought of Villi and Njál as figures connected across the centuries, the hindsight of one man enmeshed in the other man's foresight.

Villi also told me how Iceland's greatest poem, *Lilja* ("The Lily," symbol of purity), came to be written at Thikkvabaejarklaustur. "One day a terrible argument broke out at the monastery," he said. "A brilliant but hot-tempered young monk by the name of Eysteinn Ásgrímsson beat up the abbot in a moment of fury. He was locked up in chains and the trial caused great scandal. During his time in jail, he repented and wrote this beautiful poem about the Passion of Christ."

Lilja was a pioneering work in terms of poetic language and metric: one hundred stanzas, each stanza eight verses, each verse eight syllables. Most Icelanders read it in school and keep a copy of the book at home.

Thikkvabaejarklaustur was a wealthy monastery. "It owned rich agricultural lands and it had extensive rights to gather driftwood along the coast," Villi told me. "There were as many as a hundred and forty farms nearby with whom the monks had regular dealings. These were sheep farms in the main, but the farmers grew corn and coarse oatmeal for their horses. In those days the monastery was by the water. The supply of fish was very plentiful, and so were game and bird eggs. The fishermen who cast their nets in the Kutha Fljot used *currachs* made of calfskin or sealskin, similar to those in which monks had sailed over from Ireland in the early days. The skin was pulled tight and tautened with tallow and the vessels were very seaworthy. There was a nice harbor in the Kutha Fljot. Many ships spent the winter there. They were mostly Norwegian merchants, but later, when the Norwegian realm went into decline, they came from Germany and especially England. They made their way up here at the end of the fourteenth century and established commercial links. They wanted a piece of the cod trade. They came for cod and they would spend the winter."

I asked Villi about the hot springs Messer Nicolò described in his letter. "They may have dried up or gotten clogged up long ago," he said. "There have been so many volcanic eruptions over the centuries in this region that the terrain has changed a great deal."

The wind had picked up. It was getting dark but the lights in the house were still switched off. I asked Villi why he didn't keep any sheep on his farm.

"I had plenty before I retired a few years ago. And cows and pigs and of course hens. The Icelandic hen was brought over by the first settlers around the year nine hundred. It is still with us," he chuckled. Some years back it had been on the verge of extinction and Villi happened to own the very last of the Icelandic roosters. One day he got into his pickup truck and drove to Reykjavik with his rooster and he handed it over to the Ministry of Fisheries and Agriculture so they could breed it. That's how Villi saved the Icelandic hen.

The old farmer kept talking even as he faded in the darkening room. I could barely make out Arna anymore, a mere shadow sitting opposite me. Her long silences told me she was so absorbed by Villi's stories that she was forgetting to translate.

The vintage dial phone rang with a shattering suddenness. Arna managed to switch the light on. Villi's large hand groped for the receiver, and it was only after he had fumbled a good long while that I realized the old man was blind.

He spoke briefly on the phone. "It was Thordur," he said, putting the receiver down with two hands. "He wanted to make sure that you had come by to see me." He laughed. "As you can see I have friendly neighbors who take good care of me."

CHAPTER SIX

Estotiland, Drogio
and Icaria

AFTER SPENDING the summer in Iceland, Messer
Nicolò rigged up his ships and headed back south.*
According to Nicolò the Younger, he did not make it
through the following winter: "Being unaccustomed to the
bitter cold, he fell ill and died soon after returning to Frislanda." But Nicolò the Younger was mistaken: it turns out
Messer Nicolò did not die in the North Atlantic after all. His
paper trail in the Venetian archives shows that he was back in
the city by the end of 1387. He did not stay idle very long. In
January of the following year, he accepted the post of commandant in Methoni and Koroni—the two eyes of the
Republic on the western coast of the Peloponnese. He continued to serve the country in a variety of offices, but his reputation, as I shall describe later on, was tarnished by charges
of financial misconduct; eventually he was forced to withdraw from public life.

. . .

* Nicolò the Younger writes that Messer Nicolò went on to explore
the eastern coast of Greenland before turning south, but he gives no addi-
tional information on that particular journey, and my feeling is that he
was still confusing Greenland with Iceland. However, some scholars
think Messer Nicolò may have sailed west and explored parts of eastern
Greenland before returning home.

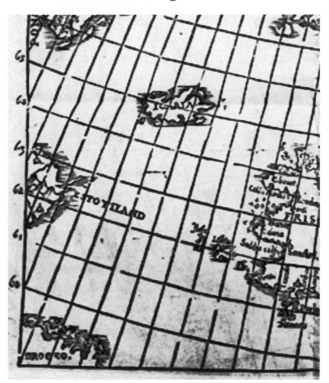

*Icaria, Estotiland and Drogeo (sic) are the westernmost out-
posts in Nicolò the Younger's chart of the North Atlantic.*

ANTONIO SUCCEEDED Messer Nicolò as commander of
Zichmni's fleet in Frislanda and stayed on another ten years,
roughly until the end of the century. Typically, Nicolò the
Younger suggested Antonio would have liked to return
sooner to Venice. "But despite all his efforts and prayers, he
was not allowed to come home because the enterprising and
courageous Zichmni was determined to become the lord of
the northern seas, and relied on him to achieve that goal."
Always the indispensable Venetian!

Antonio, the youngest of the Zen brothers, was a more
elusive figure than either Carlo, the war hero, or Messer
Nicolò, the rich merchant and navigator. I found it hard to
track his earlier life in the Venice archives. He may have been

the same Antonio Zen who succeeded Messer Nicolò as captain of the army in Romagna in 1359, but there was another Antonio Zen, a cousin, living in the city at the time, and since there was no patronymic attached I could not be certain. Perhaps he was the Antonio Zen who went to Cyprus in 1360 at the head of a merchant galley, although he would probably have been too young to lead such an important commercial expedition. There was little else to go on in the public record, suggesting he had not held important offices. Nor did he appear to have played an important role in the war against the Genoese, in which his two older brothers proved so instrumental.

I did find out he married a woman called Nicoletta; they had an only son, Pietro Dragone. After Messer Nicolò left Venice in 1383 on his journey to the Atlantic, Antonio and his young family moved into the large house at San Fantin with Messer Nicolò's wife, Fantina, and their four children: Antonio, Giovanni, Chiara and Tommaso. It was shortly after his own family had settled in that Antonio joined his brother in the north.

HENRY SINCLAIR, meanwhile, was consolidating his power in the earldom. The conflict with his cousin and archenemy, Malise, had continued to fester after the failed assault in Shetland. It now came to a bloody end.

Malise made a formal claim on the estates he was occupying illegally. The Crown rejected it in 1386. The following year Malise obtained a pardon in exchange for a vow of submission and he eventually managed to get into Queen Margaret's good graces. He and Henry were both in Denmark in 1389 to put their seal on the claim of Erik of Pomerania, Margaret's nephew, to the twin throne of Norway and Denmark—the act that put a formal end to the old Norwegian realm. Interestingly, Malise came immediately after Henry in the order of precedence, suggesting his standing had risen considerably with Queen Margaret.

Shortly after his return to Shetland, Malise and several of his cohorts were ambushed and brutally murdered at Tingwall, the valley in the heart of Mainland, where the old Viking chiefs used to meet for their assemblies. It is impossible to say with certainty whether Henry had him killed. But in Shetland lore, it is generally assumed that he did.

During my visit to Shetland, I drove out to Tingwall along an old and narrow road that wound its way through the vale. The place had probably not changed much at all since the time of Malise's murder. On one side of the road were several silvery lochs teeming with wild duck and guillemot; on the other, green hills and sheep. It was a beautiful drive, and it was easy to miss the rough-hewn block of granite that was said to mark the place where Henry's cousin was hacked to death. It stood about eight feet high, right by the side of the road, and was entirely covered with green and grey lichens. There was no inscription, no sign of any kind—just a weather-beaten stone standing tall in the ancient landscape.

AFTER HIS murder, Malise's estates went to his only surviving aunt, Isabella Sinclair—Henry's mother. To make sure that he would inherit all Malise's possessions at Isabella's death, Henry then convinced his brother, David, and his sister, Elizabeth, to renounce the rights to their share in exchange for several estates in Scotland.* In this way Henry strengthened his family's position vis-à-vis the troubled Norwegian kingdom while maintaining a relative independence from the Scottish crown. Antonio wrote home admiringly that "Zichmni was worthy of immortal memory as much for his courage as for his statecraft."

.   .   .

* Isabella survived all her children, including Henry; the earldom and all her estates were inherited by her grandson, William Sinclair.

IN THE Zen narrative Antonio came across as an able and loyal second in command, one who probably thrived in the shadow of greater men. But he was also eager to leave his own mark, as his more charismatic brothers had already done. When the opportunity arose to lead an ambitious expedition across the ocean, he pursued it with enthusiasm.

In a letter to his family, Antonio wrote that a fisherman had made his way back to Frislanda after spending many years in rich and fertile lands across the ocean, and that his story was causing great excitement among the population.

Nicolò the Younger assured the reader he was faithfully reproducing the fisherman's tale as Antonio related it in his letter. "I have merely substituted some archaic expressions and changed the style a little here and there," he said. But his hand was perhaps busier than he let on, especially as he neatly embedded the fisherman's tale within the larger story of the Zen travels. In fact, his use of the "tale within a tale" technique throughout the book may have been a way for him to give rhythm and structure to the narrative while masking the lack of verifiable facts.

The fisherman's tale itself generated so much controversy in later years that it deserves to be given in full. What follows is my translation of Nicolò the Younger's version.

The Fisherman's Tale

"FOUR FISHING BOATS went out to sea twenty-six years ago. They were caught in a storm and lost their way. When the storm finally abated after many days, one of the boats came in sight of an island called Estotiland, about a thousand miles to the west of Frislanda, and made a landing. The six men aboard were taken by the islanders to a beautiful and populous town. The king summoned his interpreters. None could understand the language of the foreign fishermen, save for one, who had been shipwrecked on the island some time before and spoke a Latin tongue. This man asked the six fishermen who they were and where they came from; he then repeated everything to the king, who asked that the men remain in the country. The fishermen did as the king wished, for they had no choice but to obey. They stayed five years and became familiar with the local language. One of them in particular (the fisherman who returned to tell the story) traveled to different parts of the island and says it is very rich in all manner of goods and is not much smaller than Islanda, but much more fertile as it is irrigated by four rivers that come down from a high mountain.

"The people who live there are very ingenious, they have much the same skills we have and have developed the same crafts: indeed it is believed that at some earlier time they traded with Norsemen. The fisherman says the king had several books in Latin, which none of the natives could understand. Their language and alphabet are quite peculiar. They mine different kinds of metals, including gold, which they have in great supply. They trade with Greenlanders, importing furs, hides, sulfur and pitch. It is said that to the south there is a great country, very populous and very rich in gold. They grow wheat and make beer, a common beverage among northern people, as wine is with us. They have extensive woodlands and they are skilled in the art of stonemasonry and there are many communities and defensive fortifications. They are shipbuilders and sail the oceans but they do not have the use of the magnet and cannot locate the north with a compass.

"The six fishermen were much appreciated by the king; he sent them with twelve of his own boats down the coast to a country called Drogio. They were assailed by a storm and thought to be lost at sea. They had, in fact, survived, although having escaped a cruel death, they ended up suffering an even crueler one: they were captured and eaten by a ferocious indigenous people who not only fed on human flesh but considered it a very savory dish. Only one fisherman was spared, so he could teach them the secret art of fishing with nets. Every day the fisherman went out with his nets, at sea or up rivers. He caught plenty of fish and gave his catch to his captors, who became more friendly. In time, he was much honored and beloved. Indeed his fame spread to nearby populations. One chieftain grew so desirous of having him by his side to witness his wondrous skill with his fishing nets that he declared war on the other chieftain. He was more powerful and better armed, and so prevailed, and the fisherman was sent to him. In the course of the thirteen years he spent in the region, the fisherman claims he was sent to no less than twenty-five chieftains, for they made war on one another just for the privilege of having him on their side. So the fisherman moved from place to place and he came to know the land well. He says the country is big, a new world as it were, but it is inhabited by very primitive people who lack most of our finished goods and go about naked despite the bitter cold—indeed they have not learned to cover themselves properly with the furs of the animals they hunt. They do not use metals of any sort, they live off game and carry arrows made of wood with sharpened points and bows the strings of which are made of hide. These are ferocious people who fight one another to death and even eat one another. They have priests who enforce the laws, which change from tribe to tribe. But the more one travels south the more one sees signs of civilization. The climate is more temperate and there are cities and temples to the idols where men are sacrificed and eaten. Gold and silver are highly valued in these southern regions, where goldsmiths and silversmiths are very skillful.

"Many years passed. His companions had given up hope of ever seeing their country again* but the fisherman yearned to return home. He bade them farewell, fled into the woods and headed back toward Drogio. At first he stayed

---

* Here Nicolò the Younger contradicts himself, having just written that all except the fisherman had been gobbled up by the natives.

with a neighboring chief, who knew him and held him in great esteem and so treated him well. Going from one chief to the next, he made his way back and after a long time and many travails he eventually reached Drogio. He lived there for three more years, until one day several boats arrived from abroad. He went to the shore and asked where they came from and was told they came from Estotiland. He asked to go back with them and they were glad to take him on board. He was useful as an interpreter for he knew the language of Drogio well. For some time after that he traveled between Drogio and Estotiland. He became wealthy and so was able to build himself an oceangoing ship. Finally one day he rigged it up and sailed back to Frislanda, bringing back news of this rich country."

THE FISHERMAN'S tale intrigued historians and geographers as soon it was published. Some praised it as one of the earliest descriptions of the New World and others ridiculed it as pure fiction cleverly assembled by Nicolò the Younger with material pilfered from travel narratives circulating in Venice during his time.

Despite the fabulous tone of the story, the central premise—that a group of fishermen was storm-driven across the Atlantic Ocean and shipwrecked somewhere along the North American coast—was not in itself remarkable. In late medieval times fishermen from Portugal, the Basque region, France and England began to sail across the ocean to harvest cod off the banks of Newfoundland. Storms were frequent and fishing vessels were lost at sea as a matter of course. A shipwreck along the coast of North America was certainly a possibility.

In rewriting the fisherman's tale for contemporary readers, Nicolò the Younger no doubt ennobled the text with references to antiquity—an element of style that was typical of the Renaissance. He transformed the fisherman into a Ulysses-type hero who, characteristically, lost his way in a storm and survived the strangest adventures before finding his way back home. It seemed to me the story was bathed in an early version of magical realism, brought into fashion by the narratives of discovery of the mid-sixteenth century.

Frederick Lucas, a nineteenth-century critic who denounced Nicolò the Younger as a shameless liar, was convinced that the fisherman's tale was an adaptation of Jerónimo Aguilar's vivid account of his shipwreck in Jamaica in the early sixteenth century,* a copy of which would have been available in Venice.

It is possible Nicolò the Younger took a look at Aguilar's story. There were other sources of inspiration as well. Benedetto Bordone's *Isolario,* a book on the geography of islands published in Venice in 1528, included, in addition to information on the cannibalistic practices of native Americans, a specific reference to "a very high mountain from which four rivers flow into the plain dividing the country"— a landscape suspiciously similar to the one mentioned in the fisherman's tale.

Nicolò the Younger was certainly not shy about embellishing, adjusting, rewriting and even plagiarizing other texts in order to make the fisherman's tale more credible. The concept of plagiarism we have today did not exist in the sixteenth century. There were no copyright laws and "importing" material was simply one of many accepted narrative techniques. And Nicolò the Younger would certainly have felt compelled to insert a few elements to bring the story up-to-date. For example, the passing evocation of the Aztec Empire

---

* Jerónimo Aguilar sailed to America with Juan de Valdivia, the Spanish conquistador. They were shipwrecked off the coast of Jamaica and twenty men drifted to the coast of Yucatán in a small boat. Most were dead by the time they touched land. The survivors were captured by the Mayan people. Five of them, including Valdivia, were sacrificed at a feast and their bodies were devoured. Aguilar was to be sacrificed at the following feast and was held in a cage with a companion. The two managed to escape and they surrendered to another Mayan chief who took them on as slaves. Hernán Cortés, who freed them in 1519, during his first expedition to Mexico, employed Aguilar as an interpreter during his conquests.

to the south—where the climate was warmer and civilization more advanced, where there were cities and temples and where men were sacrificed and eaten, where gold and silver were highly valued—seems lifted straight from the conquistadors' reports on the land of Montezuma.

Despite the evident tampering on the part of Nicolò the Younger, the fisherman's tale contained exciting new information. The place-name "Estotiland," for one. The exact origin of the word was unclear; it may simply have been Nicolò's sloppy transcription of the word "Escotiland": a land discovered or claimed by Scots. But the mistake was never corrected and Estotiland survived as a geographical entity well into the seventeenth century. One finds it marked in clear capital letters on all the important maps, usually across the maritime provinces of present-day eastern Canada.

Nicolò the Younger placed Estotiland on the western edge of the Zen map, three degrees to the south of the tip of Engronelant. Did he see it as an island along the North American coast or as a part of the American continent? Even among the strongest believers in the authenticity of the Zen map there has never been a consensus about the true identity of Estotiland. The English geographer R. H. Major (1873), for one, was convinced it was Newfoundland because its description "fairly agrees" with the latter and its size is "a little less" than Iceland. But Giorgio Padoan, a Renaissance scholar in Venice, more recently concluded (1988) that Estotiland was in fact Nova Scotia, just south of Newfoundland, because it was the only place in the region which was both heavily wooded *and* rich in gold fields.

Whether it was Newfoundland or Nova Scotia or even other parts of Labrador, the "natives" encountered on Estotiland do not appear to have been an indigenous people. As the fisherman reported, they had European skills, they traded with the Norse colonies of Greenland, they extracted minerals and they were familiar with the craft of masonry. They sowed wheat, brewed beer, built ships and, tellingly, had never seen a magnet compass.

Was the fisherman describing a vanishing Norse community on the North American coast?

Twentieth-century archaeologists have brought to light much valuable information about the Norse presence in North America during pre-Columbian times. Today the fisherman's description of the people living in Estotiland seems more intriguing than outlandish. But in 1558, when Nicolò the Younger published his book, the memory of the Greenland colonies and the Norse expeditions to North America had been erased. No one living in Venice in the mid-sixteenth century was aware that since early medieval times Viking settlements in Labrador, Newfoundland and possibly Nova Scotia were the farthest outposts of a transoceanic trade route that stretched from Norway to Iceland to Greenland, and all the way to the North American coast.

The Icelandic sagas tell the epic story of the Greenlanders' journeys to North America in pre-Columbian times. Around AD 1000 Leif the Lucky, son of Erik the Red, sailed up the coast of Greenland and then across the Davis Strait. He reached Helluland—the Land of Rock Slabs (Baffin Island?); sailed down to Markland—the Land of Forests (Labrador?); and eventually reached Vinland—the Land of Wild Grapes (Newfoundland?). He spent the winter on the North American shore before returning to Greenland. In 1960, Helge Ingstad, a Norwegian explorer and archaeologist, discovered a Norse site in L'Anse aux Meadows,* on the northern tip of Newfoundland. The settlement was built around AD 1000 and may well have been where Leif and his companions spent the winter.

The Greenland Vikings failed to colonize the region, possibly because of the hostility and overwhelming force of indigenous tribes. But they continued to cross over to North America in the summers to stock up on precious timber with which to build their houses and ships back home. They were also on a quest for iron—indeed, they may have obtained

---

* From the French L'Anse aux Méduses, Jellyfish Bay.

their crude iron blooms by refining bog iron directly in North America (a pit furnace was found at L'Anse aux Meadows). And the Greenlanders took advantage of the mild summer climate and the rich wildlife on the North American coast to hunt black bear, lynx and marten, which they skinned to make warm furs for the freezing winter months back home. With time, they probably ceased going as far south as Nova Scotia and Newfoundland and limited their expeditions to Labrador and Baffin Island. In 1972 Deborah Sabo, an archaeologist excavating Thule Inuit ruins on Baffin Island, dug up a haunting little ivory figure depicting a Norseman wearing a long tunic and a cross on his chest. It was carbon-dated to the thirteenth or fourteenth century, when Viking "commutes" to North America were slowing down. Their last recorded trip across the Davis Strait took place in 1347, when a ship left North America, lost its way in a storm and weeks later reached the coast of Iceland, having missed Greenland entirely. It is conceivable, however, that one or more small Viking communities in North America not unlike the one described in the fisherman's tale survived a few years after communications between North America and Greenland had effectively ceased.

In this scenario, the presence of a Latin Bible on Estotiland was not an absurdity. Greenlanders were Christianized around AD 1000 and clergymen joined a number of Viking expeditions to North America. Bishop Eirik Gnupsson, Greenland's first bishop, crossed the Davis Strait in 1121 to bring comfort and spiritual guidance to stranded members of his flock.

What could have worried Bishop Eirik so much that he should embark on such a daring mission? In those days, the Church was obsessed with the issue of consanguinity, and the problem of intermarriage was clearly very acute in isolated Norse settlements. The issue was so serious that the archbishop of Trondheim reported to Pope Alexander III that on an island "some twelve days away from Norway" parishioners were so closely related that they could not marry according to canonical rules. The archbishop wanted to know what he was to do about it.

Although in the thick of his struggle with the Holy Roman Emperor Frederick Barbarossa, Alexander III, the "lawyer-pope," took time out from his daily woes to craft a carefully worded response to the archbishop. He was willing, he wrote, to give dispensation in cases of fifth, sixth and seventh degree consanguinity, but in no way should it be extended to the fourth degree, i.e. between first cousins. And only if the archbishop was "absolutely certain that the people are in such great difficulty on this account."

The pope and the archbishop did not name the place, but they were probably referring to an island or region settled by Norse people on the North American coast. Had they been speaking of either Iceland or Greenland, they would naturally have used the Latin names for those islands, both of which had tax-collecting bishoprics and were well known to the Roman Curia. But in speaking of an island "twelve days away from Norway," they probably meant twelve days away from the Norse realm, which extended to Greenland. And since it took approximately twelve days to sail up the coast of Greenland to Disko Bay, cross the Davis Strait and follow the current down the coast of Labrador, it is possible that the "island" that worried the archbishop and the pope may indeed have been Newfoundland.

THE LAND of Drogio, like Estotiland, made its first appearance in cartography by way of the fisherman's tale quoted in the Zen narrative, and was soon a fixture in all the major maps of North America of the sixteenth and seventeenth centuries. The etymology of the name has remained a complete mystery. Geographers can usually be counted on to offer their bit of wisdom on the origin of names, but not in this case. A baffled Richard Henry Major told the Royal Geographical Society in 1873, "Subject to such sophistications as the word may have undergone in its perilous transmission from the tongues of Indians via the Northern fisherman's repetition, to the ear of the Venetian, and its subsequent transfer to paper, Drogio appears to have been a native name for an extended tract of North America." What the original native name might have been, Major did not say. More recently (1974), Frederick Pohl wrote that "Drogio" was more likely to be the Italian-ized form of a Scots Gaelic word. He suggested *droch*, mean-ing evil, or *drogha*, a hand fishing line.

The fisherman said Drogio was a "country," not an is-land; how large a country he did not say. Nor did the Zen map, drawn by Nicolò the Younger a century and a half later, clarify the size: only Drogio's notched contour protruded from the left side of the chart, below Estotiland. Geogra-phers generally associated the term with the coastal region of New England. The fisherman—they speculated—could have been taken in by some Algonquin tribe along the coast and then forced to move inland, from one warring tribe to another, deep into Iroquois territory, before eventually mak-ing his way back to the coast.

The tale made much of the natives' taste for human flesh, and indeed most tribes in northeastern America engaged in some form of cannibalism. Also, coastal tribes fished mostly with hooks and lines—while nets and net sinkers did not appear until the fifteenth century and may have been intro-duced by European fishermen. But Nicolò the Younger, writing in Venice in 1558, would not have had any contem-porary source to rely on for information about the north-eastern tribes: the first reports did not appear until after Samuel de Champlain's travels in the region in the early sev-enteenth century. Therefore some of his information may well have come, as he claimed, from Antonio's letter home.

Indeed, if the fisherman's tale remains so compelling it is precisely because it reflects Nicolò the Younger's ingenuous attempt to blend two visions of the world, one medieval (drawn mostly from his damaged family papers) and one the product of the Age of Discovery (drawn from the reports of Renaissance explorers and navigators). In the medieval vision, which is vividly apparent in the Zen map, Estotiland and Drogeo (*sic*) are the farthest appendices of the known world. In the more modern vision, perhaps better captured in the narrative, Estotiland and Drogio have become the gateways "of a country very large, a new world as it were."

No medieval writer would have used the expression "new world"—a catchword of the Age of Discovery. Clearly it was planted in the text by Nicolò the Younger.

THE NARRATIVE says Antonio's imagination was fired up by the fisherman's tale. After spending close to a decade in Zichmni's service in Frislanda, he longed to set up an expedition to the mysterious regions on the other side of the ocean. So he was understandably excited when Zichmni suggested that he should lead such a party. He set about planning the expedition, assembling the fleet, making sure the ships were in good order, stocking provisions for a long journey. He wrote to his brothers in Venice that the enterprise was generating such anticipation that he did not expect any difficulty in recruiting good hands: "Many are those who wish to come aboard for the sheer novelty of the voyage. I believe we shall assemble a strong crew of volunteers without having to spend public monies to hire men."

The old fisherman himself was meant to come along as chief guide, but he died a few days before departure—"a bad omen," Antonio commented. He was replaced by other mariners who had sailed back with him from Estotiland. With a hint of disappointment, Antonio also informed his brothers that Zichmni had decided to lead the expedition himself, while he had been relegated to second in command.

At last the fleet departed, setting a northwestern course. It paused in the Faroes to stock up on water and dried fish. Zichmni avoided further stops and sailed directly out in the open sea to take advantage of favorable winds. But very quickly a great storm gathered strength and the ocean turned "into a sea of gloom." The tempest was relentless.

Day after day the ships were "battered and thrown about." They drifted apart in the maelstrom until they lost sight of one another. Many ships went down. The others battled on in furious winds, crashing against towering sea walls. The sky loomed over them so dark and menacing that the men could not distinguish day from night, "and we never knew where we were." After eight long days of "great torment" (*travaglio*), the mighty storm finally subsided. Part of the original fleet managed to regroup and continue on its journey westward until it sighted land.

"As we reached what seemed a safe and quiet haven," Antonio went on in his letter, "we saw a large number of natives crowding the shore, armed and ready to strike at us to defend the island. Zichmni instructed all of us to show peaceful intentions. The natives sent over ten of theirs, who spoke ten different languages; we understood none of the men except one, who said he came from Iceland. The man was brought before Zichmni, who asked to know the name of the island and its ruler."

At this point Antonio's tale took a baffling turn into mythology. "The man said the name of the island was Icaria, and all the kings who ruled the island were called Icarus, like the first king, who was the son of Daedalus, king of Scotland. Wishing to sail further, Icarus had left his son behind to rule the island in his absence in accordance with the laws that are currently in use there. But Icarus perished in a great storm and this is why to this day they call their sea the Icarian Sea."

Nicolò the Younger claimed he was quoting Antonio's letter verbatim, but this was not the language of a fourteenth-century Venetian merchant—his fingerprints were all over this section of the story.

Icaria, of course, was the island of Ancient Greece named after Icarus, son of Daedalus, the clever Greek architect who designed the labyrinth for Minos, king of Crete. Out of favor with Minos, Daedalus fashioned a pair of wax wings for himself and his son Icarus in order to fly to Sicily. But Icarus flew too close to the sun. His wings melted, and he fell into the sea and drowned. His body washed ashore on an island that was named after him to remind everyone of the perils of human hubris.

I could not understand why Nicolò the Younger had chosen this bizarre variation of the Icarian myth—and with a Scottish twist no less! But references to antiquity appeared frequently in sixteenth-century travel narratives and charts, the River of the Amazons being perhaps the most famous example. The use of imagery borrowed from Ancient Greece was not just a literary device; it was probably a way for the author to gloss over his own confusion about the new geography.

It occurred to me that Icaria might be Nicolò the Younger's distorted transcription of Acadia, the old name for Canada's maritime region. Some linguists say the place-name was derived from *caddie/quoddie*, a word used by native tribes to designate a fertile region. But others say it is not derived from a native term at all and that it was introduced into the language by Giovanni da Verrazano in 1524: while sailing north of the Chesapeake Bay, he called the coastal region Arcadia because it brought to his mind the pristine beauty of mythical Arcadia—again Ancient Greece! Then the "r" was dropped when Verrazano's diaries were transcribed, and Arcadia became Acadia or Acadie, as the French possessions along the coast of Canada were known.

In any case, the Icaria that was floating in the Zen map between Engronelant, Estotiland, Frisland and Islanda appeared to be a sizable island. Geographers have claimed it was everything from county Kerry in Ireland (Richard Henry Major) to St. Kilda, the last of the Hebrides (Frederick Lucas). But Zen devotees have usually identified Icaria as Newfoundland—albeit a Newfoundland that had clearly drifted much too far out into the ocean.

LET US get back to the scene on the crowded shore. The throng of natives stood there facing down Zichmni and his men. They wore nothing but shabby animal skins and kept their bows and arrows at the ready. "The interpreter told us the natives were satisfied with their God-given state and did not wish their lives to change," Antonio wrote, describing the tense encounter. "For this reason they did not welcome foreigners. They wished to warn Zichmni against any temptation to break their laws, adding that we would face certain ruin because they were ready and willing to lose their lives to protect those laws."

Despite their hostile attitude, the natives conveyed through the interpreter their curiosity about the newcomers. They asked Zichmni to leave one of his men with them, assuring him that he would be well treated. According to Antonio, the Icarians were especially keen to have one of the Venetians stay on with them "so they could learn our language and our customs just like they have learned those of other countries from the ten or so foreigners who live among them."

The passing reference to the "foreigners" living among the natives brought to my mind the later adventures of the French navigator and explorer Jacques Cartier. Stopping in Newfoundland on his way to and from the St. Lawrence in the 1530s, he spoke to the natives and recognized a number of words from European languages, including Breton, Gascon, Provençal, Catalan and Italian. Today we know that fishermen sailed from Europe to fish off the Grand Banks in the fifteenth century; the words Cartier recognized were probably traces left by those fishermen in Newfoundland. But it may be that European fishermen reached Newfoundland as early as the fourteenth century, which would account for the "foreigners" mentioned by Antonio.

Zichmni reacted prudently in the face of the natives' overwhelming force—there is no mention that he left any of his men on the island, Venetian or other. After gathering as much information as possible on the topography of the island, the coastline and the natural havens where he might weigh anchor and attempt another landing, he ordered his crew to set sail and move on. But as soon as he thought his small fleet was out of sight, he reversed course and followed the coast until he found a bay suitable for landing. The men went ashore "in great hurry" to gather driftwood and fetch fresh water. But a few natives living in the area saw the Europeans and alerted their fellow tribesmen with smoke signals. Soon a large number of them, heavily armed, appeared right above the landing site. "They rushed down to shore shooting arrows and killing and wounding many of our men," Antonio wrote. "There was no point in our trying to make peace with them: the more the battle raged on, the fiercer and crueler they became. We were forced back onto the boats and out of the bay." They rounded the cape and sailed south, always hugging the shore. Zichmni wanted to attempt one more landing to replenish the stock of supplies before taking to the high seas. But the natives were relentless. "A vast and well-armed multitude continued to follow us on land, passing over rivers and mountains. As we rounded another cape pointing north, we found ourselves trapped in treacherous waters filled with sandbars and bristling shoals. For ten days we could not extricate ourselves from that dangerous sea and often risked losing our fleet. Fortunately, we had very fine weather. As we rounded the easternmost cape, we saw more natives at the top of the cliffs and along the shore. They shrieked and yelled and continued to fling arrows from a great distance. Their hostility showed no sign of abating. We nevertheless decided to find a good harbor and make one last attempt to communicate with them. It was all in vain, for the people—in this they were truly like wild animals—never laid down their weapons and showed every intention of fighting us to death if we attempted a landing. Zichmni saw that if he persisted in his attempt, we would soon find ourselves without supplies. As the wind finally picked up the fleet headed out to sea."

If Zichmni and his men were indeed leaving Newfoundland behind, their contact with the North American continent was limited to that hurried landing to gather driftwood and fresh water. In 1497, a full century later, another Venetian, John Cabot,* reached Newfoundland aboard the *Matthew* after searching in vain for a shortcut to China. Although he made history, Cabot's foray ashore was just as hasty, for he feared being eaten by the natives. After quickly planting the banners of the king of England and of Saint Mark, he rushed back on board and sailed to England, where Henry VII awarded a prize of £10 "to him that found the New Isle." Four years later his son, Sebastian Cabot, returned to Newfoundland and this time stayed long enough to round up three natives who were "clothed in beast skins and ate raw flesh and spoke such speak that no one could understand" and brought them back to England.

All that was in the future. Zichmni, meanwhile, was apparently in no hurry to return home. His fleet sailed northwest for six days (i.e., toward Labrador). Then the weather changed and a strong southwesterly breeze—Antonio used the Venetian word *garbino*—started blowing in the direction of Greenland.† "The sea grew rougher but for four days we

---

* John Cabot (Giovanni Caboto), born around 1450 in Genoa, moved to Venice with his family when he was still a boy and became a Venetian citizen in 1476. He traveled to the eastern Mediterranean and became a skillful navigator. He moved to London around 1484. Like many great seamen of his day he was obsessed by the notion of finding a northwestern passage to Cathay. News of Columbus's discoveries prompted Henry VII of England to authorize a voyage from Bristol to search for new lands. After one aborted trip in 1496, he sailed again in 1497 and reached Newfoundland in the mistaken belief that he had reached the northeast coast of China. A second expedition in 1498 was probably lost at sea.

† Frederick Pohl says the fleet sailed in a southwest direction, and after four days reached Nova Scotia. He goes on to assert that Zichmni/Henry Sinclair established a base camp in Nova Scotia, entered into a close relationship with the Micmac Indians, and went on to explore the coast of New England. This reading of the Zen narrative forms the basis for the claim that Sinclair was among the first Europeans to explore North America. A few years ago members of Clan Sinclair unveiled a memorial in the shape of a Viking ship's prow on a hill overlooking Guysborough Harbour, at the end of Chedabucto Bay, in northeastern Nova Scotia. And at Halfway Cove, a few miles up the road, the Prince Henry Sinclair Society of North America has placed a fifteen-ton granite boulder to commemorate what the society believes was the actual landing place of the expedi-

managed to sail fast before the wind until at last we sighted land. We made our approach warily because the sea behind us was in great turmoil and the land we had reached was unknown to us."

---

tion. Pohl's interpretation with regard to the direction taken by the fleet can be traced to an erroneous translation in the first English edition of the Zen narrative, published in London in 1616 by Hakluyt, who described "the wind changing to the Southwest." Two centuries later, in the second English translation, Richard Henry Major repeated the error ("the wind changing to the south west"). But the original Italian text is clear: the wind was blowing *from* the southwest and the fleet was sailing ahead of the wind in a northeastern direction, toward Greenland.

CHAPTER SEVEN

Engroneland

T HE WESTERN coast of Greenland was so sparsely populated at the end of the fourteenth century, the landscape still so pristine, that at first glance a mariner might well have believed he was coming into un‑ charted territory. There were no hostile natives crowding the shore to repel the intruder, no villages in sight along most of the coastline, no immediate sign of human presence. But a bird's‑eye view of the territory would have shown the new‑ comer that he was not alone. The Inuit, who had first migrated to Greenland from the north some three thousand years earlier, had advanced all the way down the coast, to the southern region, where the last of the Norse settlers lived a precarious existence in a few scattered farms—all that remained of the once prosperous colony founded by Erik the Red.

The sagas say that Erik, or Eirik as he was known, an Ice‑ landic outlaw, sailed west around AD 980 looking for land sighted by stray navigators and made landfall on the eastern coast of Greenland. He then headed south and, rounding the cape, discovered that the climate was warmer and the terri‑ tory more hospitable on the western coast. After spending three years exploring fjords and meadowlands, he sailed back to Iceland to recruit more settlers. He called the coun‑ try he had discovered Greenland, for he thought that men would be much more eager to go there if the place had an attractive name. The marketing trick worked: as many as twenty-five ships sailed with him although only fourteen arrived at their destination.*

Erik settled at Brattahlid, a pleasant tract overlooking Eiriksfjord (today's Tunulliarfik) with rich pastures for raising sheep and cattle. Archaeologists digging at the site have uncovered a large farmstead with at least three major buildings scattered in grassy fields filled with bluebells and poppies that slope to the edge of the water.

The other settlers established farmsteads in nearby fjords. The land was good and the fishing waters and hunting grounds were plentiful. More Icelanders migrated to Greenland in the following decades and the Norse colony eventually grew to have a population of about 6,000. The Eastern Settlement was actually in the lower part of the western coast and occupied an area that went roughly from Brattahlid down about a hundred miles to Herjolfsnes. The smaller Western Settlement—where the population, at its peak, was about 1,500—developed further north, near the area of today's capital, Nuuk.

Sometime in the twelfth century the Norse settlers began to interact with the Thule Inuit; they called them *skrælings*—"scruffy wimps." The Thule Inuit were themselves, in a manner of speaking, newcomers to Greenland, having migrated from Alaska and Canada sometime between AD 900 and AD 1000. Theirs was the third great migration from the north. The Saqqaq Inuit had settled in Greenland as early as 2500 BC, followed by the Dorset Inuit around 700 BC. Nearly two thousand years later, the Thule Inuit colonized the eastern coast of Greenland, then moved down the western coast, eventually coming into contact with the Norse settlers, who were pushing north in search of new hunting grounds.

During the heyday of the Norse settlements, in the twelfth and thirteenth centuries, Greenland was an impor-

---

* There are two sources for Erik the Red's story, *The Greenlanders' Saga* (c.1200) and *The Saga of Erik the Red* (c. 1265).

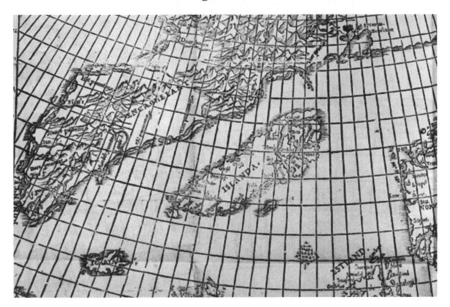

Detail of the Carta da navegar *published in 1558 by Nicolò the Younger showing Engronelant (sic). It was the most accurate depiction of Greenland published until that time.*

tant link in the trade chain that stretched across the North Atlantic from Norway to North America. Greenlanders specialized in exporting exotic luxury goods to Europe: narwhal horns, walrus tusks, polar bear and white and blue arctic fox furs, and the prized white falcons for which European and Arab princes paid extravagant prices. Other staples were dried caribou meat, walrus and seal skins, cod liver oil, seal blubber, eiderdown and the coarse warm wool spun and woven by Greenlandic women during the long winters. Greenlanders traded their goods for iron and pitch as well as malt and honey. They had a great need for timber as there were no trees in Greenland, but in time it became simpler to mount logging expeditions to Labrador than to wait for ships carrying Norwegian wood.

Greenland became the Church's westernmost outpost. A bishop's see was established at Gardar in 1124 and a cathedral was erected there around 1200. In all, five churches were built in the Eastern Settlement, as well as a Benedictine nunnery and an Augustine monastery, and two more in the Western Settlement. Most of these buildings have long disappeared and only a few large stones that formed the outer wall of the Gardar cathedral remain in place. At Hvalsey however, which is a day's walk from Gardar, the four walls of the old church are still standing on a steep hill overlooking the fjord. One can easily picture the old Norse folk from nearby farmsteads gathering for Sunday Mass as the bells ring out festively.

The decline of Norway in the fourteenth century gradually brought trade with Greenland to a halt. As fewer and fewer ships arrived, the Greenlanders turned inward, living off their products and their meager trade with the Inuit. Inevitably, the Church lost touch with its remotest flock. After Bishop Alf died, about 1378, at the time of the Great Schism, several bishops were named to replace him, but none made the trip out to Gardar. With the onset of the Little Ice Age, the five-century-long cooling period that took place roughly from the fourteenth to the nineteenth centuries, climatic conditions worsened steadily and farms struggled to survive in an atmosphere of gloomy isolation.

In her novel *The Greenlanders,* Jane Smiley movingly describes the decline of one family in the vanishing Norse colony. The story begins in the second half of the fourteenth century. The winters get colder, food becomes scarcer and a series of diseases—the "coughing illness," the "vomiting illness," the "joint illness"—further decimate the dwindling population. Family feuds weaken the community and the chieftains eventually cease to participate in the Thing—the yearly assembly. Even the Church, once an aggregating force in the Greenland colonies, degenerates into an agent of division. And then, one day, Bristol ships sail into Eiriksfjord. English marauders come ashore and go on a rampage. They desecrate the cathedral in Gardar, kill the churchmen, rape the women and steal all the food they find, dealing a deadly blow to a doomed community.

Smiley tells a haunting and plausible tale, but no one really knows what caused the end of the Norse colonies. Perhaps a sudden calamity—a contagious illness, a severe famine—wiped out the last generations of enfeebled Greenlanders. Their extinction might have been accelerated by the encroaching Inuit population. It is also conceivable that some of the last settlers sailed off to Labrador looking for a new start. But nothing has surfaced so far to reveal the chain of events that snuffed out a community of intrepid settlers that survived on the outer edge of the western world for five centuries. What is certain is that by AD 1500 the last Greenlanders had all but buried one another; nothing remained of the once prosperous colonies but crumbling farmsteads and a couple of old churches.

Smoky Mountain

ZICHMNI'S EXPEDITION reached the southwestern coast of Greenland "at the start of June," Antonio reported. The fish were plentiful in the coves along the coastline and the sky was full of seabirds. The apprehension the men had felt during their approach was soon replaced by an eagerness to disembark and explore the rolling meadowlands. "The air was sweet and temperate. There was no one in sight and we began to think that this agreeable place was uninhabited. So we named the harbor Trin and the land that went out to sea Cape Trin."

Trin was most probably shorthand for Trinity, a frequent choice of name among travelers. Holy Trinity, a religious feast established in 1334, occurs between mid-May and mid-June. It so happens that in 1398, the year in which the expedition allegedly took place, it fell on June 2, a date that fits well with Antonio's statement about arriving in Greenland in early June. Where was Cape Trin? Nicolò the Younger placed it at the bottom tip of Greenland—today's Cape Farvel. But nothing in the narrative indicates its location and, as far as I know, they could have landed anywhere along the southwest coast.

SHORTLY AFTER landing, Antonio went on to write, "We saw smoke coming out of a mountain in the great distance and this gave us hope that the place was inhabited after all." Zichmni dispatched one hundred of his soldiers and told them to bring back news about the smoky mountain and the people who might be living in the region. Meanwhile, the rest of the army established a base camp and gathered supplies of water and driftwood. The famished men caught plenty of fish and seabirds in the nearby fjords and found large quantities of eggs on which "they immediately gorged themselves."

After eight days, the soldiers returned, having reached the mountain and encountered many natives, "short creatures, half savage and fearful, who quickly retreated to their cavernous dwellings as soon as they saw our men." Thule Inuit were hardly timorous people; on the contrary, they were brave, highly skilled fishermen and hunters who thought nothing of going out in their kayaks to chase a whale in freezing, turbulent waters. Nor were they encountering Europeans for the first time: they were used to bartering with the Norse settlers in the south. In fact, a retreat in the face of a hundred-strong detachment of fierce-looking, well-armed foreign soldiers sounded more like an act of prudence than one of cowardice. But it was a common enough view among geographers and cartographers of the sixteenth century that the *skrælings* in Greenland were a small and fearful people; or, as Bordone put it in his *Isolario,* "pusillanimous dwarfs no more than a cubit high." Thus Nicolò the Younger may well have tinkered with Antonio's description of the natives to make it fit with the contemporary image of the native Greenlanders. Indeed he may have made up the entire reference to the *skrælings* in order to make the narrative more credible. Sources of inspiration on that topic were certainly not lacking in Venice. In his *Historia de gentibus septentrionalibus,* the book of reference for the North Atlantic in Renaissance Europe, the Swedish prelate Olaus Magnus devoted an entire chapter to "pygmies" in Greenland (*"De pygmaeis Gruntlandie"*). In 1554, only four years before Nicolò the Younger came out with the Zen narrative, Gerard Mercator, the great Flemish cartographer, published his influential map of Europe. Across southern Greenland was the following inscription: *"Hic habitant Pigmei vel Screlingen dicti";* "Here live pygmies, also known as skrælings." In order to write about Greenland in an informed, up-to-date manner, Nicolò the Younger would have had to mention a description of the "pygmies" living there; even if Antonio had said nothing about them, he probably would have felt entitled to illuminate the reader by adding a few sentences himself on the matter.

More intriguing than the description of the pygmies, in my view, was the explanation the soldiers gave for the smoke billowing out of the mountain. "Inside was a great fire," Antonio reported, "an incandescent fountain as it were, from which a dark, gurgling pitch-like substance oozed out of the mountainside and streamed down toward the sea." The words were precise and carefully chosen. They were the result of on-the-ground observation, and they made it plain that what the soldiers were confronted with was *not* some sort of volcanic activity, as the reader might have been inclined to believe, but some other natural phenomenon. Indeed there are no volcanoes in Greenland—active or extinct. So what exactly did Zichmni's men find on their reconnaissance mission?

The mystery of the smoky mountain baffled experts[*] until the 1970s, when the director of the Geological Survey of Greenland, Knud Ellitsgaard-Rasmussen, came up with a

---

[*] Frederick Pohl, believing the Zichmni expedition sailed to Nova Scotia instead of Greenland, came to the conclusion that the smoky mountain was Mount Adams, on Nova Scotia's north shore, facing the Strait of Northumberland.

possible explanation. Just north of Disko Bay, on the western coast of Greenland, there is a one-hundred-mile-long peninsula called Nugssuaq that stretches out into Baffin Bay in a southeast-northwest direction. Midway along the southern coast of the peninsula Ellitsgaard-Rasmussen located an area that the Inuit called Pujortoq — the smoky mountain.

Unlike the rest of Greenland, which is mostly made up of solid black basalt that is billions of years old, the Nugssuaq peninsula was formed by cretaceous and tertiary sediments only millions of years ago. The ground is still geologically young and unsettled. Just beneath the surface are layer upon layer of self-igniting bituminous shale. As some of the mountains along the fjord are very steep, the layers of shale continually slide and chafe against one another, generating intense heat and smoke.

Nuuk

I WENT TO GREENLAND hoping to find Pujortoq. In Copenhagen, I took the daily Air Greenland flight to Kangerlussuaq, a converted World War II U.S. Air Force base once known as Bluie West 8. A prop plane then flew me to the capital, Nuuk (population 15,000), a small town on the western coast with a big industrial harbor linked to the fish-processing plants and crowded with open-jawed Royal Arctic cargo ships.

Nuuk's main street threads its way between round slabs of granite on which small wood-framed houses are perched precariously. I passed by a pizza parlor, a Chinese restaurant, a couple of clothes shops, a bank and a hotel. The largest building was the post office. The fishmonger's shack was on the way out of town. Three wrinkled-faced Inuit women in fisherman's boots, each with a cigarette dangling from her toothless mouth, hovered over the daily catch: a half dozen decapitated seals lying one next to the other like human corpses laid out after battle.

Beyond the town center were rows of spray-painted concrete tenement houses with broken doors and smashed windows. The tourist office found me a room with an elderly widow of mixed blood. She worked at the fisheries and spent the evenings at home sewing colorful Inuit ceremonial clothes for her granddaughters.

AFTER THE Norse colonies died out around 1500, Europeans ceased to come to Greenland, and for more than two centuries the Inuit had the place to themselves. The Danish kingdom, meanwhile, inherited the old Norse realm. In the eighteenth century, the Danes returned to Greenland to develop a whaling and fishing industry, and from 1721 onward they governed the island harshly.

After World War II a slow process of emancipation began. Greenland became part of the Danish Commonwealth in 1953 and home rule was granted in 1979. My brief stay in Nuuk coincided with a referendum on the issue of self-government, the next step in Greenland's slow move to independence from Denmark. The population today is made up of some 58,000 Greenlanders, most of Thule or mixed extraction, like my landlady, and only 6,000 Danes. Still, Greenlanders I spoke to told me they were hesitant about moving to full sovereignty. They liked the idea in principle and hoped their vast deposits of natural resources would bring them wealth. But they also feared the consequences of going their own way—chief among them the loss of Denmark's 3.4 billion kroner yearly subsidy.

"Many of us are nervous about losing all that money," Inga Dora Markussen, the young editor-in-chief of *Atuagagdliutit*, Greenland's daily paper (circulation 2,800), conceded in her light-filled office above the post office. "I doubt that drilling and mining Greenland's resources will lift Greenlanders out of chronic unemployment. The population is very sparse and scattered along the coast. The workforce has very little mobility—Greenlanders don't like to leave their family or their village. We would simply be invaded by foreign workers." Half Greenlandic and half Danish, Inga Dora said that, like most Greenlanders, she favored a cautious "no rush, no risk" approach to full emancipation. "We will become independent at our own pace, whenever we are ready."*

According to Daniel Thorleifsen, the burly, soft-spoken director of the Greenland National Museum, the threat to the national heritage was a more pressing issue than independence. "We are the last products of the Thule culture and we still have a lot of archaeological work ahead of us if we want to understand the history of our people," he explained to me when I visited the museum—a little red cottage in the old colonial harbor that the Danes built in the eighteenth century, when Nuuk was still known as Godthåb. Thorleifsen said the archaeological program was actually benefiting from rapid climate change because important Thule sites were becoming more accessible than in the past. But global warming was also making Greenland more attractive to large multinational oil and mining companies that were muscling their way into the country. "We are engaged in a race against time," he warned. "And my concern is that we shall not be able to salvage the archaeological treasures that have yet to be mapped."

I mentioned to Thorleifsen my own rather more improbable archaeological quest. He graciously conceded that he had never heard of the Zen voyages and directed me to Hans Lange, an archaeologist whose office was down the hall. Lange, a Greenlander from Ilulissat, in Disko Bay, knew nothing about the Zen brothers either. But he perked up when I told him I was looking for a place called Pujortoq. "Ah, the smoky mountain on Nugssuaq," he said. "I have

---

* The referendum was held in November 2008 and approved by 80 percent of the voters; with self-government came legal ownership of Greenland. Greenlanders are now entitled to move on to the final stage of emancipation, full independence, according to their own timetable, but early enthusiasm was dampened by the worldwide economic slump.

never seen it myself but I have heard about it." Lange suggested I travel north to Ilulissat, an old whaling station formerly known as Jakobshavn, and then take the weekly post boat up to the Saqqaq settlement on Nugssuaq. "There you might find someone who can help you."

To Pujortoq

THERE IS NO SCENIC Route 1 up the breathtaking coast of western Greenland. To reach the Disko Bay area from Nuuk one must either take the slow-going post boat or fly back to Bluie West 8 in Kangerlussuaq and wait for the next prop to Ilulissat. The Greenlandic winter was already in the air, time was running out and I had no choice but to fly. As I boarded the plane to Kangerlussuaq I recognized the pilot who had flown me into Nuuk a few days before. "Jens Larsen," he said, shaking my hand. He was a friendly, jovial man, with a broad smile and just a hint of a swagger. He had come out from Copenhagen twenty years before to fly helicopters. "I'm still here," he said, laughing.

Ilulissat turned out to be a small frontier town at the end of the Kangia Glacier. The view looking out to Disko Bay was breathtaking. Icebergs floated placidly in the silver-grey sea like sculptures in a water garden. Disko Island rose clearly to the west. The Nugssuaq Peninsula lay a hundred miles to the north and on a good day its outline was visible to the naked eye. The town of Ilulissat was formed by a collection of small bright red, blue, yellow and green houses built on hard, lichen-covered basalt. I found a room in the back of a saloon-type establishment at the main crossroads, with a melancholy view of a muddy back alley; I unpacked my few things and went for a walk. It was not long before I heard a booming voice coming out of a curio and travel shop. A man was yelling in Greenlandic, but the accent was distinctly Italian. I stepped in and peered into the back office. The voice belonged to a short, barrel-chested man with a thick black mustache; he was tapping furiously on his computer key-board and shouting cooking instructions into the mike of his headset.

Silverio Scivoli was known to everyone in town as Silver. He had came to Ilulissat thirty years earlier as a pianola player touring Inuit country and had fallen in love with Marie, a native girl. He stayed on, they had four children, and he never went back to Italy—where he still had a wife and two sons.

Silver showed me a bag full of frozen caribou steak and chunks of arctic hare. "I never liked hunting in Italy," he said, "but in Greenland I love going out into the wild with a gun." As he spoke, it occurred to me that no matter how far one travels the odds are one will bump into an Italian, and he will be planning a meal.

Silver informed me I had just missed the weekly post boat that serviced the Disko Bay region. "Come back tomorrow," he said. "I will find someone who will take you to Nugssuaq Peninsula."

To my disappointment, he did not ask me to dinner.

Instead, I had coffee and a ham sandwich with Jens Larsen, the pilot. He and his family lived down in Nuuk but he still owned a small house by the water down at the old harbor of Ilulissat; he had purchased it back in the eighties, when he had come out as a very young pilot to fly Air Greenland's Sikorskys to his heart's content. "After work, when the weather was good, I would grab my fishing rod and fly my chopper to some beautiful, wild spot, fish some trout, make a fire and spend the night under the stars and be back for work early next morning." Air Green-land no longer ran chopper flights up and down the coast and Larsen was stuck with prop planes on the Nuuk-Kangerlussuaq-Ilulissat route. But each summer he took his family on a flying trip to Europe in a refitted World War II bomber plane he kept in a hangar in Germany. "I pack the wife and kids and we take off on a random journey," he said with a laugh. "The plane is heavy so we fly very low over beautiful countryside and scare the wits out of the cows and the sheep."

Larsen had just returned from Europe and was happy to be back. "I love it out here," he said. I asked him what he thought about Greenland's slow march to independence. "I wish them good luck," he answered wistfully.

THE NEXT day I packed a light lunch and went for a walk, following a trail out of Ilulissat that went over a hill and then sloped down toward the Kangia ice fjord, to the stone ruins of a three-thousand-year-old Dorset Inuit settlement. The stones were scattered in a natural amphitheater overlooking a bay of staggering beauty where celestial ice formations were on grand parade. Occasionally, the ceremonial silence was broken by the distant drone of a fishing boat or the startling crack of an iceberg.

I pulled out a tuna sandwich and a cool Greenlandic beer from my rucksack and settled down for a pleasant lunch among the Dorset ruins. The sun came out and the icebergs glittered in the bay. I could hear the gentle lapping of the sea on the pebble beach below so I walked down to the clear water and ran my fingers through it. I quickly took my clothes off and splashed about, gasping for air at the cold.

On the way back to town the fields were covered with gentians, angelica, wild rhododendron and beautiful arctic poppies. There were patches of sweet, succulent blueberries everywhere, and each time I knelt down to pick a handful I smelled the juniper and thyme that grew around the basalt outcroppings. It occurred to me they would have made good seasoning for Silver's roast.

I heard the sound of children at play coming from the next valley, and when I reached the top of the hill I saw them scurrying about in their red and blue and yellow jackets. Their teacher had brought them out for the afternoon to pick berries for Christmas cakes and gather moss for the crèche. I pointed out that it was only mid-September. "Soon there will be snow on the ground and ice and it will be too late," the teacher said. "We must think ahead."

On the way home, I counted more than a hundred winter shacks spread out in the drab outskirts of Ilulissat. Peeling sleds rested on the roofs; rows of cod hung from fish racks like dirty linen left out to dry. Around each shack, ten to twelve sad-looking sled dogs lay chained in the dust, longing for the first snowfall. There must have been at least a thousand dogs lying around, but I was not immediately aware of their number because they faded into the grey landscape. One pack of hounds got up and shook off their late-summer torpor, letting out a plaintive wail just as I passed by. Soon all the sled dogs in the valley joined in until the howl was so deafening I felt I had to quicken my pace.

"THIS MAN will take you north to Nugssuaq," Silver said in his baritone voice when I checked into his shop. Christian was another Greenlander of mixed heritage—a Danish father and an Inuit mother from the village of Saqqaq, on the Nugssuaq Peninsula, where he still had a few relatives. He was a quiet man, unusually tall and broad for a Greenlander. His no-nonsense manner inspired confidence. We arranged to meet the next morning at the harbor.

The following day it was raining and the fog was low and I feared we would have to cancel our plans. But Christian, as promised, was down at the harbor filling up two extra tanks of gasoline for the hundred-mile journey up the coast to Nugssuaq. His boat was impressive: a Glastron Bowrider with a 300 horsepower Mercury outboard engine, which he had picked up in Nuuk and driven solo up the jagged coast of western Greenland. He threw me some extra-warm clothes, a wool hat and ear protection and I bundled up. Despite the rain, the sea was calm and the icebergs perfectly still. Ice floes were scattered as far as the eye could see. Christian zigzagged between them with great assurance.

Along the way, we stopped at Rodebaye, a small fishing

village. At the bay's entrance, on a basalt ledge, the carcass of a blue whale had been picked to the bone by local fishermen. Among the shacks that lined the water's edge was a small house painted bright red where a dour German couple served us cabbage and whale meat.

As we cruised north the air cooled. It stopped raining and the fog lifted, revealing a bleak arctic landscape. The sea became choppier after we passed Crown Prince Island, as the fast-moving current of the Sullorsuaq Strait ran into the placid waters of Disko Bay. At last we reached the Nugssuaq Peninsula and pulled into the small, ramshackle harbor of Saqqaq. There were two dozen houses scattered haphazardly, a general store and no one in sight. Christian moored his Glastron to a rickety wharf. Then he turned to me and asked, "What is your plan?"

I had no plan, so I suggested we look for his cousins. Christian grunted and we headed for the village. He told me he used to spend his summers in Saqqaq when he was a kid but hadn't been back in many years. We knocked on several doors looking for his relatives until we found them inside a pale blue house on a hillock, staring into a large television screen.

After a round of greetings, we sat down for coffee. All of them had heard of the smoky mountain. Pantomiming the scene, they said the smoke was like the clouds of vapor that shoot out from the back of a whale. But when I pulled out a map of the region and asked them to point out its location, each cousin put his finger in a different place.

"I know where it is," said a young man who had been sitting alone in an armchair nursing a backache. "I have been to the mountain." His name was Tchichus. "One day I was fishing up near Pujortoq and I landed my boat on the rocky beach and climbed halfway up the mountain," he said, pulling up his chair. "I was frightened by the noise and the heat, and the smoke was suffocating me so I ran back down and I never returned."

Tchichus said the mountain was roughly fifty miles up

the coast. He did not want to take us there on account of his bad back and his bad memories of the place. And I sensed Christian was not going to risk navigating his way up an unfamiliar, shoal-infested coast without Tchichus's assistance. It was getting late, the temperature was dropping and I was losing hope of reaching our destination. Then Christian walked over to his cousin and after a brief exchange Tchichus perked up. A few minutes later the three of us were back in the Bowrider. Christian said it was a good thing we had brought extra gasoline. I asked him why his cousin had changed his mind and he grinned: "I told him he could drive my boat on the way back."

We moved upstream warily because the canal was full of insidious reefs that were often hidden by ice floes. But we had a great view of the wide plains between the ranges. The field grass had yellowed and the turning leaves of willow brush and blueberry gave the landscape a rich, rusty color. The only sign of human presence along the coast was an isolated hunting lodge—a tiny white dot in an empty valley. "We use it in the winter," Tchichus said. "As soon as the canal freezes over we ride up from Saqqaq on our dogsleds and hunt deer and caribou."

The map indicated that Pujortoq had an altitude of 1,905 meters, but when we came in sight of the mountain, the smoke coming out from the wide openings on the side and center blended with the fast-moving clouds, obscuring the view. Still, it appeared to be far more massive than I had expected. When we got closer I realized it was formed by three mountains, with two dark cleavages down which streams of boiling hot bitumen ran to a wide beach made of small, angular black rocks. Tchichus indicated to us the route he had attempted to follow up the mountain. I could see why he had fled in terror: the mountain was alive and threatening as the burning layers of shale shifted and chafed in its underbelly.

We bobbed about while I kept peering at the mountain through binoculars. What was I looking for? I had reached my destination. I had found a smoky mountain. I had made my point. Yet I did not want to let go of that unsettling presence, perhaps in the hope of some final revelation.

The waves were getting bigger. Christian was worried about crashing the boat against the rocks. He nodded to me and we slowly turned away.

Tchichus was relieved; he took the helm with a big smile and rode the waves back to Saqqaq, swerving between shoals and ice floes. We dropped him off on the pier and I watched him fade in the gloaming as he waved good-bye with one hand and held his aching back with the other. Darkness was falling quickly and we still had a hundred miles to go before reaching home. The clouds were low and navigating across the ice fields in the dark was dangerous. "Every minute counts," Christian said abruptly. The feeling of safety that had enveloped me since we had left Ilulissat in the morning abandoned me in a rush of adrenaline. As we headed into that gloomy sea, wet and shivering, I wondered for the first time whether I had not gone too far, putting myself in danger for the sake of an old Venetian tale.

But the clouds cleared after a short while and a shiny moon brightened the arctic night. The cold air seared my lungs. I felt safe again in Christian's capable hands as he deftly steered his boat. Along the way, luminescent icebergs hovered over us like friendly ghosts. And before long, I saw the twinkling lights of Ilulissat in the distance, straight ahead of us.

Return to Frislanda

ONCE THE MEN HAD SAFELY returned to the camp after their expedition to the smoky mountain, Zichmni announced his desire to establish a proper camp in order to explore and map the country. "The air was clean and clear," Antonio explained, "and the land and the rivers were good." But the men began to grumble: "They were tired of traveling and many wished to return; they complained that winter was getting closer and that if they waited any longer they would not be able to leave until the following summer. In the end, only those who wanted to stay did so. They kept the large rowboats for themselves. The others were sent back with most of the sailing ships." It made sense for Zichmni and those who stayed behind to keep most of the large rowboats, which were better suited than the sailing ships for navigation along the coast and deep into the fjords (although he must also have kept at least one and possibly more sailing ships with which to make the return journey, as they could not have built them in Greenland for lack of trees).

Antonio was not to take part in the exploration of Engroneland. "Against my will," he added wistfully, "[Zichmni] asked me to take command of the fleet that was returning home." He took advantage of strong prevailing westerlies and after twenty days of smooth sailing along the sixtieth parallel—the usual route for mariners sailing east— he veered to the south. After another five days he finally saw land. It was the island of Neome (which Nicolò the Younger placed midway between Frisland and Estland on the Zen map). "I knew the island and realized I had traveled beyond Islanda," Antonio wrote. "Having replenished our stock of supplies, we sailed with good winds and in three days reached Frislanda, where the people greeted us with great joy."

When Zichmni returned to Frislanda, possibly as early as the following year, he reported to Antonio that he had managed to chart "both sides of Engroviland [sic]," i.e., the eastern and western coasts of Greenland. Antonio must have copied and sent a chart to Venice because a century and a half later, Nicolò the Younger, usually so imprecise in his mapmaking, used it to draft the most accurate map of Greenland available in those years, not just in Venice but anywhere in Europe.

After more than a decade spent in Zichmni's service, Antonio was now ready for the long journey home. In his last letter from Frislanda, he wrote to Venice telling his family he was coming back at last and was bringing with him a book in which he had written down his experiences during the years spent in the north: "I describe in it the countries, the monstrous fish, the customs of the men, the laws of Frislanda, Islanda, Estlanda, the kingdom of Norway, Estotilanda [*sic*], Drogio, and the deeds of our brother Nicolò, the Chevalier, and his travels to Grolanda."

The book included an account of "the life and deeds of Zichmni," a man "of great valor and goodness" whom Antonio had grown to admire. Roughly fifteen years had passed since Zichmni had saved Messer Nicolò and his Venetian crew from the hostile natives after their shipwreck in Frislanda. The book Antonio had put together "and which God willing I shall bring home with me" was the magnificent result of that providential encounter.

"I will add no more," Antonio wrote at the end of his letter, anxious to embrace his brothers, his wife, Nicoletta, and his son, Pietro, now a grown boy, "as I hope to be with you soon and to satisfy your curiosity about these and many other things with my own voice."

CHAPTER EIGHT

Squaring the Circle

I DOUBT Antonio ever made it back to Venice. I found no trace of a new political or military appointment, no lease of a galley, no deed or official document of any kind, not even a death certificate. Only an indirect reference to him turned up in the archives, which confirmed that he was no longer living in May 1403, when his wife, Nicoletta, bought a Tatar slave and signed the contract as Antonio's widow (*"relicta ser Antonii Zeno"*). The most plausible explanation is that he died of some illness or accident or else perished in a storm at sea during his homeward journey. The book that he was carrying and was so eager to show to his family presumably disappeared with him.

A good deal more is known about Messer Nicolò's inglorious end. We left him in 1388, as he sailed off to his new duties in Methoni and Koroni, in the Peloponnese. But he was back in Venice the following year, then went off to Treviso to witness the formal act of submission of that city to the Most Serene Republic. He returned to Venice as ducal counselor and in 1391 he headed out once more to the Peloponnese, taking with him his wife, Fantina, and their youngest son, Tommaso. Two years later rumors spread in Venice about some financial wrongdoings on his part. The rumors found their way into official reports, and the prosecuting magistrates started a formal investigation in October 1394. Messer Nicolò was tried in absentia (his son Giovanni testified in his defense) and was found guilty of embezzlement. In January 1396 he was interdicted from public office and ordered to make full restitution and pay a fine of two hundred ducats.

Messer Nicolò never recovered from the blow. He withdrew to the island of Murano in the Venetian lagoon during the period of interdiction and in 1400 he wrote his final will, leaving most of his possessions to Fantina and his children. I was not able to find a death certificate for him either, but he must have died within the next three years because the family had the will authenticated in 1403.

It was not the end of the troubles for the Zen brothers. In 1404 Carlo, the popular hero of the war against the Genoese, was accused of having taken bribes during that conflict from a Paduan lord who had sided with the enemy. Carlo was found guilty, although he appears to have been the victim of political machinations. He spent two years in jail and then went on a pilgrimage to the Holy Land. After his death, in 1418, the Republic reversed the record on his earlier conviction and honored him with a state funeral. Thereafter Venetians revered him as a national hero.

Messer Nicolò and Antonio, on the other hand, soon faded into obscurity. Their voyages in the northern seas did not open the way to new Venetian trade routes. The state convoys to London and the North Sea went into decline as Venice forsook its maritime vocation to expand its influence on the Italian mainland. In fact, Messer Nicolò's oldest son, Giovanni, leased one of the last Venetian galleys to travel to London and Flanders, in 1401, suggesting that in the Zen family at least, the lure of the north was strong until the end.

CARLO'S AND Messer Nicolò's bloodlines died out, and it was Antonio who ensured the Zens not only survived into the following generations but prospered for several more centuries.

Antonio's son Pietro, known as the Dragon in honor of his grandfather, was, like many of his ancestors, a merchant in the Levant. He married Doge Morosini's niece Anna and died in Damascus around 1425. Pietro's son, Caterino, became something of a celebrity. He too traded in the east, and amassed a small fortune; he then made an excellent match by marrying Violante Crespo, daughter of the duke of the Greek archipelago. In 1470 the Venetian government sent him to the court of Uzun Hasan, the king of Persia, to try to draw him into a war against the Ottoman Empire. In Persia, Caterino was treated as a member of the royal family (which indeed he was: the king's wife was Violante's aunt) and he stayed two years, eventually persuading Uzun Hasan to take up arms against the Turks. Upon his return to Venice, he received a hero's welcome and lived out his retirement in a large house with a garden he bought on Fondamenta Santa Caterina.

Caterino's son, Pietro, built up a successful trade with Constantinople, where he befriended Suleiman the Magnificent. Not surprisingly, he became a strong advocate for peace with the Ottomans and was very influential in shaping Venice's eastern policy during the dogeship of Andrea Gritti. At the end of his long life, wishing to enlarge the house he had inherited from his father, he bought several adjoining buildings on the same block and set about integrating the various properties into a single palazzo large enough to accommodate his four sons: Francesco, Caterino, Vincenzo and Giovambattista.

The new building ran the length of the entire block. It was designed by Pietro's first son, Francesco, with the help of Sebastiano Serlio, an influential Renaissance architect living in Venice at the time. Francesco died in 1538, shortly after construction began. The next year, Pietro, the eighty-four-year-old patriarch, followed his son to the grave. In his will, he instructed his three surviving sons to complete the façade of the palazzo according to Francesco's drawings, while leaving them free to arrange and decorate the interiors of the building as they wished. The will also specified that the façade and the sides of the palazzo were to be adorned with frescoes of scenes from the family history. The commission was given to Tintoretto, then a promising twenty-year-old artist.

In the archives of the Museo Correr in Venice I found a sketch of the floor plan showing the three-way partition of the palazzo. Vincenzo moved into the central body; Giovambattista into the western wing. Caterino, the eldest, took over his father's old apartment, in the eastern wing, with his wife, Gabriella Querini, and their four children: Vincenzo, Ottaviano, Elena and Nicolò the Younger.

I imagine this was where the letters and charts of Messer Nicolò and Antonio finally came to be stored after being moved around from one Zen residence to another down the generations, and where Nicolò the Younger gathered what remained of those old and tattered documents to piece together his book.

Having returned to Venice after my own journey to Frislanda, as it were, I made my way back to the crooked old palace on the Fondamenta Santa Caterina, this time to linger on the narrow embankment, nose up in the air, to take a better look at the decrepit façade.

The palazzo, which no longer belonged to the Zen family, was divided into many apartments. It had an unusual architectural style that combined elements of Venetian Renaissance and Gothic revival. But there were deliberate oriental touches that seemed designed to reflect the family's long association with the Levant. I was struck by a decorative frieze that ran under the high cornice along the length of the façade. It was so blackened by soot that it was impossible to make out the motif from where I was standing. Giovanni Sarpellon, the amiable Venetian gentleman who lived on the top floor, was kind enough to invite me up to his apartment. Leaning precariously out of the window of his living room, I observed up close a lovely relief of small chariots, palm trees, gazelles and camels loaded with merchandise—an oriental scene no doubt familiar to successive generations of Zens. But farther down the cornice, the frieze took on a

The original group of medieval houses (at center, facing the canal) purchased by Caterino Zen and his son Pietro on Fondamenta Santa Caterina. They were torn down and replaced by Palazzo Zen in the sixteenth century.

marine-life motif with large fish—dolphins? whales? cod?— leaping about in perfect symmetry. And I wondered—on the basis of nothing but my own fancy—whether these might not be a reference to the Zen voyages in the northern seas.

The external frescoes, painted by the young Tintoretto and his collaborator, Andrea Meldolla, had long been erased by time and humidity. Indeed, the walls had peeled so thoroughly in the previous five centuries that only the crumbling brickwork was visible. But the building was more protected on the far western side, and above a window on the *piano nobile*, a small patch of dark pigment—perhaps the last fragment of the original fresco—dotted the wall like an age spot on a crinkled old face.

The marble plaque honoring Messer Nicolò and Antonio

for their travels in the northern seas was on the corner of the eastern wing, beneath the window of what must have been Nicolò the Younger's apartment. The nineteenth-century tablet had been covered with soot when I had seen it the first time, but someone had apparently come to clean it in the meantime because the marble slab was now quite resplendent and the script clearly legible.

NICOLÒ THE Younger never became the historian he had hoped to be. The book on the Zen voyages was the last he published. Perhaps the mysterious disappearance of his longtime printer, Marcolini, had something to do with the end of his writing career—shortly after the publication of the Zen book, Marcolini traveled to Verona and was never seen or heard of again. It is also possible that the oppressive

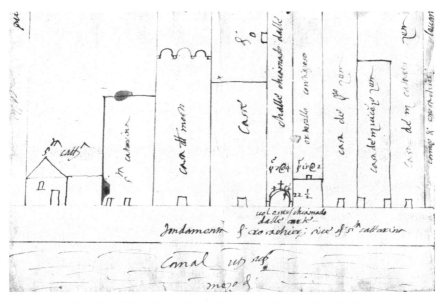

Sketch of the floor plan of Palazzo Zen as divided up
by the three surviving Zen brothers after the death of Francesco.
Caterino Zen and his son Nicolò the Younger lived in
the apartment on the far right.

atmosphere of the Counter-Reformation discouraged Nicolò the Younger from pursuing his literary ambitions. Whatever the case, he put aside his writing projects and concentrated on his career as a public servant.

After a lifetime in government, he reached the highest echelons of power, thanks to a succession of high-profile appointments in defense and land management—his two areas of expertise. In 1564 he turned down the governorship of Cyprus in order to remain in Venice, apparently to stay near his dying wife. The following year he was appointed to the Council of Ten, the secretive heart of executive power in the Republic. Before the year was out, however, his health took a turn for the worse and he died "after twenty days of high fever," at the relatively young age of fifty.

Nicolò the Younger's book on the Zen voyages, on the other hand, went on to enjoy an unexpectedly long life, stirring up controversy for the next four and a half centuries. Its early appeal is easy enough to understand. Here was a travelogue about a region of the world that had yet to be properly explored and mapped, a region that could prove to be the gateway of a northwest passage to Cathay—that Holy Grail of Renaissance navigation.

The book came with an added attraction: a map of the North Atlantic that showed islands and regions never seen before. Map mania was then at its peak, not just among professional cartographers but among general readers as well. Unprotected by copyright, thousands of maps and charts were copied, modified or simply picked for their choicest parts. So the inclusion of the *Carta da navegar* in the back of the book is bound to have pushed up initial sales.

However, as the Age of Discovery wound down in the second part of the sixteenth century, cartographers gradually unveiled the true outline of the world. The initial fascination with Nicolò the Younger's map would probably have faded if a copy had not traveled from Venice to the German town of Duisburg, just over the Rhine, and found its way to the cluttered workshop of Gerard Mercator.

A New Ptolemy

The year is now 1569, a little more than a decade after the Zen map was first published. The most eminent cartographer of his time is putting the finishing touches to the great achievement of his career: the first complete map of the world. It is a beautiful piece of work. Mercator has glued together eighteen separate sheets into a very large map measuring roughly six and a half feet by four. The drawings are done with great artistry and the lettering is impeccable. In fact, the whole composition is a feast for the eyes in addition to being a cartographic marvel.

The outline of Europe, Africa and Asia—the regions that constituted the old Ptolemaic world—are drawn with relative accuracy. The New World, on the other hand, still appears as if through a disfiguring lens, with North America

In the early 1560s, the great cartographer Gerardus Mercator received in Duisburg a German translation of Nicolò the Younger's book on the Zen voyages.

billowing like a huge cloud out of Aladdin's lamp while beneath it, South America is shriveled and shapeless.

At the top center of the map, between the Old and the New Worlds, one is suddenly on very familiar ground: Greenland weighs down from the Arctic over Estotiland; right below it is Frisland; Drogio and Icaria make their appearance as well. Mercator has inserted all the major pieces of the Zen puzzle in his map, rearranging them slightly in order to squeeze them all in.

I believe this single act on the part of the man many regard as the founder of modern cartography goes a long way towards explaining the extraordinary influence ("and so unwarranted!" I can hear the critics exclaim) that Nicolò the Younger's simple *Carta da navegar* had on the history of mapmaking.

MERCATOR WAS born Gerhard Kremer in a small river port south of Antwerp in 1512. His father, Hubert Kremer, was a poor tenant farmer who supplemented his meager income by working as a cobbler. After his death, in 1526 or 1527, Uncle Gisbert, a minister, became young Gerhard's guardian. He sent him to an elite school in Brabant and then to the University of Louvain, where Gerhard latinized his name to Gerardus Mercator. He studied mathematics and astronomy with the great Gemma Frisius and took on cartography to support his growing family—in 1536 he had married Barbara Shelleken, a girl from Louvain, and they had six children.

Mercator sold his first globe in 1535. He produced a beautiful map of the Holy Land in 1537. The next year he made his first attempt to piece together a world map, and followed that with a map of Flanders. There was apparently no clear direction to his work, except the one dictated by commissions; his maps and globes sold well at the fairs.

After the Reformation, the Low Countries became the scene of intense religious violence. One day Mercator was

dragged away from his workshop and thrown in jail as a suspected Lutheran (we do not know whether or not he was; he
always kept his religious beliefs a secret). He was released
thanks to his academic connections, but not before seeing
several of his prisonmates go to their deaths: two were
burned at the stake, another was beheaded and a woman was
buried alive.

He returned to his family and his cartographical work
wary of the heavy climate of intolerance. In 1552 he left
Catholic Brabant and moved with his family to Duisburg,
across the German border, in the small duchy of Cleves-
Jülich-Berg. In 1564, the duke chose him as his official cartographer. It seemed the start of a productive time, but
religious strife once again brought death and destruction to
the region. The plague returned in 1566 to take its own grim
toll. In quick succession, he lost his daughter Emerentia, two
grandsons and his son Bartholomeus.

Mercator emerged from the depth of personal tragedy
clinging to the most ambitious plan a cartographer could
possibly conceive: to map the entire universe—the world
and the heavens—into a unified *cosmographia*. He never did
complete the mapping of the heavens. But his 1569 map of
the world was to make him immortal.

Mercator worked for years on the greatest technical
problem confronting geographers at the time: how to transfer the spherical surface of a globe onto the flat surface of a
map. Straightening the latitudinal parallels into a grid was
easy enough; the difficult part was figuring out how to space
them progressively toward the poles. He could not use cal-
culus because the mathematical formulae that would have
been necessary had not yet been devised. So he went about it
empirically, checking one by one the coordinates at which
the latitudinal parallels intersected the rhomb lines on his
globes, and transferring them onto a flat map in order to
achieve "the squaring of the circle."

Mercator's projection, as it came to be known, revolu-
tionized navigation: an ocean-crossing sea captain could

*Detail of Mercator's World Map of 1569. By inserting all the main
components of the Zen* Carta da navegar *in his own world map,
Mercator unwittingly prolonged the influence of the Zen map
on cartography.*

now draw his compass direction as a straight line between a
point of departure and a point of arrival. All he needed to do
in order to plot his course was to measure the angle it formed
with any meridian and make the necessary adjustments to
take account of compass deviation.

Once Mercator had figured out the framework of his new
world map, he diligently filled it in, drawing the continents

and the oceans in a harmonious if somewhat distorted whole. However, when it came to the North Atlantic and the northern part of the New World, he had no reliable data—no reports based on firsthand observation. Possibly under pressure from his printer and his clients, Mercator nevertheless agreed to trace the outline of that murky area that was suddenly attracting so much attention in European capitals. And he turned for help to the only cartographical source available to him: the Zen map.

The catalog of Mercator's library indicates he did not own a copy of the original 1558 Marcolini edition, but he did have a later German edition. In 1561, Girolamo Ruscelli, a well-known printer in Venice who held Nicolò the Younger in the highest regard ("an authority universally thought to have few equals in the whole of Europe"), had published his own version of the Zen map as an addendum to a new edition of Ptolemy's *Geographia.* The Ruscelli edition was snatched up by Joseph Moletius, a translator and bookseller then living in Venice, who quickly put together the German edition that ended up in Mercator's library.

It was a considerable, and uncharacteristic, leap of faith on the part of Mercator. But in a moment of pressure, he evidently chose to take Ruscelli's inflated comment about Nicolò the Younger at face value and to believe in the accuracy of the Zen map. In Mercator's defense it has been said that he relied on the Zen map because it bore the seal of approval of Giovanni Battista Ramusio. But it didn't. The story of the Zen voyages was not published in the Ramusio great travel series (*Navigationi et viaggi*) until 1574—seventeen years after Ramusio's death and five years after Mercator's world map came out. The irony is that when Paolo Ramusio, son of Giovanni Battista, finally published the Zen story (without the map) in 1574, he did so largely because Mercator had given it a patent of legitimacy by including the Zenian islands on his world map!

.   .   .

BY THE end of 1569 Mercator's printer, Christophe Plantin, had sold more than forty copies of the world map, but after the initial boom, sales quickly declined. Abraham Ortelius, the most successful mapmaker of those years and a good friend of Mercator's, brought out his own heart-shaped map of the world, complete with a full panoply of the Zenian islands. If Columbus was the first to reach the southern shore of the New World, Ortelius explained, "the North part was long ago found out by certain fishermen of the isle of Frislanda, driven by tempest on the shores thereof, and was afterwards, about the year 1390, discovered anew by one Antonio Zeno, a gentleman of Venice."

This little map, more wieldy than Mercator's, became the centerpiece of a portable little atlas, *Theatrum orbis terrarum*, which Ortelius brought out in 1570, taking the wind out of Mercator's sales. Although Mercator did not become rich, his stature grew enormously as a result of his world map. Ortelius himself acknowledged his debt to "the best geographer of our time." No doubt a little peeved by his friend's financial success, Mercator nevertheless praised him "for collecting the maps into one manual that can be bought at a small cost, kept in a small space and be carried about where one pleases."

A British Impyre

JOHN DEE WAS AT HIS HOUSE in Mortlake, on the Thames, working on the preface to the first English edition of Euclid's *Elements,* when he heard that his old friend Mercator had finally published the first complete map of the world. The two had met during their student days at Louvain, where Dee, then a Cambridge scholar, had gone to study mathematics and astronomy. They had spent much of their time together, debating late into the night about everything from the position of the magnetic pole to the abstruse mathematical formulations of Pedro Nunez, the great Portuguese cosmographer.

In the twenty years since their first meeting, Dee and Mercator had corresponded regularly, and their friendship and professional collaboration had deepened with time. Following his tour on the Continent, Dee had returned to England and established his reputation as a mathematician, a geographer and an astronomer. He was also Queen Elizabeth's favorite astrologer, famously picking the date of her coronation (January 15, 1559).

Impressed by his friend's achievement, Dee was also seized by the opportunities Mercator's world map seemed to offer his country, especially with regards to the North Atlantic. He therefore added to the preface he was writing to

John Dee, astrologer, mathematician and advisor to Elizabeth I, "declared to the Queen her title to Greenland, Estotiland, Friseland."

his Euclid (a disquisition on the practical uses of geometry) a rousing call to action. English pilots, he wrote, should take advantage of England's "most commodious situation for navigation to places most famous and rich." Indeed, they were now being "half challenged by the learned," i.e., great geographers like Mercator, to sail west to North America "and little and little wynne to the sufficient knowledge of that trade and voyage: which now I would be sorry should remain unknown and unheard of."

DEE'S LONGTIME passion for geography evolved into a keen interest in geopolitics. England, he believed, had fallen dangerously behind Spain and Portugal in the race to claim territory in the New World. The initial spurt of interest in transatlantic exploration during the time of Henry VII, culminating with John Cabot's hasty landing in Newfoundland (1497), had been followed by a prolonged lull as Henry VIII turned his attention to ecclesiastic politics and the concentration of power at home. Dee argued it was high time to catch up with the other powers by unleashing British imperial ambitions in North America. He gravitated into the orbit of powerful court figures like Francis Walsingham and William Cecil, who were stoking Queen Elizabeth's interest in oversea dominions, and he devoted the next few years of his life to building his case for a "British Impyre"—a term he was the first to use in print.

Dee had a very precise idea of what had to be done. Mercator's world map showed a clear passage north of Estotiland, a large and apparently very navigable canal that ran straight through to the Pacific and from there to fabled Cathay.* However, Dee disagreed with Mercator about the

---

* Mercator's sea-lane flowed immediately below the polar region, which was formed by four symmetrical islands, each separated from the other by a fast-flowing river that rushed into a circular polar sea. According to Mercator, the whirling water was sucked from the polar sea into the

nature of Estotiland: whereas the great cartographer from Duisburg showed it to be part of the continental landmass, Dee argued that it was actually an island. And the source for this information was none other than the fisherman's tale he found in the book on the Zen voyages—of which Dee owned a heavily annotated first edition in Italian.

Antonio Zen says in the narrative that the shipwrecked fishermen "discovered an *island* called Estotiland" (my italics). Dee believed it was Baffin Island, off the coast of northeastern Canada. "It will be universally agreed," he gloated, "how lucky I have been in this new locating of the island of Estotilant [*sic*] . . . ; or, at least how carelessly others studied the brief account of the noble [Venetians]."

Dee saw Estotiland as both the gateway to vast and wealthy territories in North America and the ideal point from which to control access to the Northwest Passage. In other words, it was a strategic objective: the key to English expansion in North America and the cornerstone of the British Empire to be. Heavily influenced by the descriptions in the Zen narrative, Dee became convinced it could easily be acquired and settled and defended and therefore rallied support for an initial voyage of exploration.

---

bowels of the earth through a giant plughole, much like an emptying bathtub. A huge, glistening black rock signaled the location of the plughole. When John Dee asked Mercator what his source for the mapping of the polar region was, he told him he had relied on a written account given to him by "a friend in Antwerp." It was a convoluted story: a fourteenth-century Flemish traveler, Jakob Cnoyen, had heard "from a priest who served the king of Norway" that a Franciscan minorite from Oxford, a mathematician and astronomer of some repute, had traveled to Greenland and beyond around 1360. Later he had "put into writing all the wonders of those islands and presented the book, which he called in Latin *Inventio Fortunatae*, to the English King [Edward III]." The book, if it ever existed, was lost, and the young friar's identity has remained a mystery. When, years later, the English geographer Richard Hakluyt again pressed Mercator about his source, he replied rather lamely: "I required it again of my friend [in Antwerp] but he had forgotten of whom he had borrowed it."

MARTIN FROBISHER, a tough, courageous sea captain who had risked his life many times exploring the West African coast, was part of a new generation of swashbuckling mariners that included Francis Drake and Walter Raleigh. They hung around Elizabeth's entourage looking for funds with which to finance adventurous missions abroad. Michael Lok, Frobisher's financial partner, was a businessman experienced in subarctic trade routes. He eventually found enough backers to finance a small expedition to Estotiland and the Northwest Passage. Several close advisers to the queen—Walsingham, Cecil, the earl of Leicester and Lord Warwick—were among the stockholders.

Dee was closely involved in planning the itinerary of the voyage. He provided Frobisher with maps and nautical instruments and tried to teach him the rudiments of astronomy, with little success—although Frobisher came from a well-to-do Yorkshire family he had only a minimal education. But Dee made sure he did not leave without a copy of the Zen map.

The fleet was very small for such an ambitious journey. Three vessels in all set sail from Ratcliffe on June 7, 1576, headed for Shetland on the way to Frislanda: two thirty-ton ships, the *Michael* and the *Gabriel*, with a combined crew of thirty, and a seven-ton pinnace with only four men aboard. From Shetland they sailed north to Iceland, where they were hit by a heavy storm; the pinnace was lost with all its crew. Frobisher continued west along the sixtieth parallel, the old Norse route to Greenland. Toward mid-July he struck the southeastern coast of Greenland, roughly at the point where a deep glacier known today as Hvitserk, the White Shirt, broke up into the sea spawning mountains of ice "rising like pinnacles of steeples, and all covered with snow." Frobisher and his men were convinced they had reached Frislanda because Nicolò the Younger had placed it at a latitude of 60° on the Zen map.

The visibility was very poor and in that misty, icy labyrinth, the two ships lost contact. The *Michael* eventually turned around and headed home while Frobisher and his crew continued west aboard the *Gabriel.* At the end of July they made landfall at Resolution Island, off the southern tip of Baffin Island—the Estotiland of the Zen map in their view. They cast about for several days in heavy fog, winding their way among bergs and floes; occasionally they managed to land on an island to collect samples to be shown as proof of possession of these territories. Among the objects brought on board the *Gabriel* was a small black rock that sparkled in the sunlight.

At last Frobisher found the opening to what seemed like a long narrow channel on the sixty-third parallel and he slowly advanced in the belief he had found the elusive passage to the Pacific. Actually, the strait—known today as Frobisher Bay—turned out to be a narrow fjord roughly 140 miles long. After eight days of navigation, Frobisher went ashore, climbed to the top of a mountain, took in the view—a maze of islands and lakes and inner seas—and returned to proclaim he had seen "a great open sea whereby to pass to Cathay and the East India." It is not clear what this "great open sea" was—it might have been Hudson Bay—but Frobisher was convinced he had seen the Pacific Ocean shimmering in the distance.

The *Gabriel* was about to resume its journey west when it was surrounded by some twenty Baffin Island Inuit who paddled up in their kayaks to trade with the strange newcomers. They came aboard, exchanged goods and interacted freely with the sailors, even climbing and swinging on the ship's rigging. Then five of Frobisher's men rowed one of the natives ashore so he could fetch his kayak and pilot the *Gabriel* to the end of the fjord. But the rowboat disappeared around a point and the five crewmen were never seen again. Frobisher's men seized one Inuit in a failed attempt to exchange prisoners. With a heavy heart, Frobisher set sail for England in late August carrying aboard a frightened Inuit, his kayak and the sparkling black rock.

In London, Frobisher was given a hero's welcome. He had apparently reached Estotiland and navigated the Northwest Passage nearly all the way to the Pacific. The Asiatic features of the Inuit prisoner were clear evidence of how close he had come to Cathay. But the Inuit died soon after arriving in England, and in the course of the winter, interest shifted to the black rock picked up on Baffin Island. After consulting several assayers who confessed to seeing no particular value in it, Michael Lok informed the queen that an Italian goldsmith, Giovanni Battista Agnello, had concluded after careful examination that the rock was, in fact, very rich in gold.

A fever suddenly swept through the court of England. In March 1577, Lok launched the Company of Cathay and had no difficulty raising £5,125 to finance a much larger expedition across the ocean, with the Queen herself as lead investor (£1,000). Increasingly responsive to the pressure of her courtiers in favor of territorial claims overseas, Elizabeth asked Dee to prepare a series of policy papers laying out the legal and historical justification for acquiring lands in the New World.

Dee had already been at work for some time on the early history of English territorial expansion in the North Atlantic. Drawing inspiration from the Arthurian myths, he argued that King Arthur first conquered Orkney, Shetland, the Faroes, Iceland and Greenland back in the sixth century. He now added for good measure his conquest of Frislanda, Icaria, Drogio and the all-important Estotiland. Dee deliberately ignored the Viking voyages and the Norse settlements in the North Atlantic, insisting that the English were there first and since no one else had been there after them, it was natural and dutiful to claim those lands for the Crown. "This recovery," Dee urged, "is speedily and carefully to be taken in hand."

While the historical justification for an imperial claim on North America was rather far-fetched, the legal argument laid out by Dee was more cogent. After Christopher Columbus's Atlantic crossing in 1492, Spain and Portugal had signed the Treaty of Tordesillas (1494): all lands discovered to the west of an imaginary line bisecting the ocean from north to south belonged to Spain, all those to the east belonged to Portugal. Dee challenged the new order, arguing that the right of possession rested on physical occupation and not merely on discovery (as stated in the Treaty of Tordesillas). Only by putting up fences, erecting buildings, tilling the soil—in other words by taking over the land and managing it—could one claim right of possession. Of course the English hadn't yet discovered much territory at all in North America, let alone occupied the land. But it was important to establish the principle according to which the Queen could now possess what "the Spaniard occupieth not."

Dee laid out his legal and historical arguments in four papers, which he presented to the Queen for her approval. In November 1577 he traveled to Windsor and had several private audiences with Elizabeth. "I declared to the Queen her title to Greenland, Estotiland, Friseland," he wrote in his diary.

The essence of Dee's four papers, which laid the foundation of the British Empire in North America, have long been known in their outline. But the actual documents were lost and it was not until they resurfaced on the market and were purchased by the British Library in 1976 that the role played in this story by the Zen voyages was fully revealed. Dee, as we know, had the original 1558 Zen volume in his library. And the least one can say is that he consulted it very closely, lifting long stretches of Nicolò the Younger's narrative, often verbatim, in order to bolster his case for a British Empire in North America. Take, for example, this passage he borrowed from the fisherman's tale:

*Concerning a New Location for the
island of Estotilant & the province of Drogio*

*Two noble Venetians, who almost two hundred years
ago named not only Estotilant, but also Friseland, closer*

*to us, and many other islands lying in the northern seas,
made them known to our men by their writings. It was
on their authority that we located Estotilant about a
thousand miles, at least, to the west of Friseland. The
inhabitants cultivate their fields and brew their beer.
Their territory is rich in woods and groves. They fortify
their many cities and castles with walls, and are familiar
with ships and navigation. Many such inhabitants are
to be found, stretching continuously well into the
interior of the territory of Drogio and occupying various
different regions. But a man traveling a long way on
from Drogio itself, in a south-westerly direction
(passing through the lands of cannibals and savage
people who go always naked, however bitter the
extremes of cold they must endure), comes to a region of
a more temperate climate and to a people knowing the
use of gold and silver and living in a civilized manner.
Here, however, they sacrifice men to abominable idols
in the temples of their cities, and afterwards feast
ritually upon their flesh. To these fishermen, journeying
for thirteen years at a stretch through a variety of
unknown lands, and experiencing great kindness at the
hands of more than twenty-five different rulers, the
extent of those regions appeared so vast that they
thought they had discovered a New World.*

Not content to plunder the Zen narrative, he proceeded
to edit and embellish it, evoking an idyllic world of gentle
meadows, pleasant streams and rich farmland not unlike the
English countryside. So keen was he to draw Elizabeth into
the project that his paper on Estotiland read like something
between a travel brochure and a real estate prospectus:

*Certain Noteworthy things about
the island of Estotilant*

*Estotilant is indeed a very splendid island which,
with the province of Drogio over against it, . . . might*

with good reason draw wise men, and lovers of the Christian state, to visit and survey it. The island is a little smaller than Iceland. It is endowed with all things necessary for the easy sustenance of human life. In the middle of it there is a very high mountain from which there flow four very pleasant streams irrigating the whole island. It is ruled over by a king who lives in a very beautiful and very populous city, and who keeps in his household interpreters skilled in various tongues. In this city there was, two hundred years ago, a famous library containing various books in Latin; however, there were at that time scarcely two people in the whole island who understood that language. The islanders themselves are very ingenious and apply themselves to all the skills of the artificer, almost as well as we do; and the Venetian nobles were of the opinion that in ancient times they had had commercial dealings with men of our culture. They have a language of their own and write it with their own characters. They have mines of all metals, but are especially rich in gold. They collect Greenland skins, sulphur and pitch, and their merchants carry these home in their ships.

Preparations for Frobisher's new journey proceeded at a quickened pace. The mission was still to explore the North-west Passage all the way to the Pacific, but Lok and his stockholders instructed Frobisher not to push farther west until his men had mined an abundant cargo of black rocks. To the *Gabriel* and the *Michael* was added the *Aid*, a mighty two-hundred-ton workhorse. The total crew had grown to some 134 men, initially including a group of convicts who were supposed to be dropped off in Frislanda to take posses-sion of the island for England (instead they were discharged at Harwich because there were too many men on board).

Frobisher reached Orkney in early June, sailed on to Shetland and continued north toward Iceland before turn-ing westward. On July 4 they reached southern Greenland.

"We made the land perfect," wrote George Best, Frobisher's lieutenant, in his account of the voyage, convinced, once again, that they had reached Frislanda since "the height being taken, we found ourselves to be on latitude 60°." "This Friseland," he went on, "showeth a ragged and high land having the mountain almost covered with snow along the coast full of drift ice, and seemeth almost inaccessible and is thought to be an island in bigness not inferior to England."

If Best had a copy of the Zen narrative close at hand, it must not have been an easy read for him because he goes on to say that Frislanda "appeareth by a description set out by two brethren, Nicholaus and Antonius Genoa, who being driven off from Ireland with a violent tempest, made shipwreck here, and were the first known Christians that discovered this land about three hundred years since." Everything in this last sentence was factually wrong. It was two hundred years, not three; the Venetians were not the first known Christians to have landed there; they had not left from Ireland; their name was not Genoa. Best's inaccuracy is not surprising: the Zen narrative had yet to be translated from Italian into English and the story of the Venetians' voyages was known only in vague and misleading terms.

The map, on the other hand, was more easily available and was a crucial cartographic instrument on this second journey as well. "[The Zens] have in their sea cards set out every part [of Frislanda] and described the conditions of the inhabitants declaring them to be as civil and religious people as we. And for so much of this land as we have sailed alongst, comparing their card with the coast, we find it very agreeable." In the face of such praise, it is no wonder the Zen map continued to hold sway among mariners and geographers.

In the end, Best's account can be appreciated for what it actually is: not a description of Frislanda but a rare glimpse of the coast of Greenland, which had not been visited by outsiders since the Norse population had been snuffed out earlier in the sixteenth century. Frobisher's men were enraptured by the scintillating "islands of ice" and marveled at their "great bigness and depth." They licked the ice and were surprised to find it "fresh and sweet to the taste." Wondering where these mountains of ice could possibly come from, Best ventured they might be "bred in the sounds there-abouts, or in some land near the Pole, and with the winds and tides are driven along the coast."

One day the ships were "lying becalmed" and the men let fall a hook without any bait. "Presently, [they] caught a great fish called a hollibut which served the whole company for a day's meat." Five leagues off the shore they did more sounding and fished out "a kind of coral almost white, and small stones as bright as crystals." Best concluded the land "may be found very rich and beneficial if it were thoroughly discovered." The Inuit were no doubt lurking in the vicinity but they did not paddle up to the ships. "We saw no creature there but little birds."

After four days and nights up and down the coast of southern Greenland they set a western course toward Frobisher Bay. Within a week they reached Baffin Island and took formal possession of the land, which they called Meta Incognita. After a futile attempt to find the five men lost the year before, Frobisher set up a mining camp on a small island off the outer coast of the bay, which he named Countess of Warwick, in honor of the wife of one of the main backers of the Company of Cathay. In two weeks the men excavated and loaded on board some two hundred tons of rocks. On August 22, before the cold set in, "we plucked down our tents," wrote Best, ". . . gave a volley of shots for a farewell . . . and every man hasted homeward."

In London, Michael Lok, Frobisher's financial partner, was busy gathering funds for the next expedition as rival assayers were called in to take a look at the rocks brought back from Countess of Warwick Island. But the results were disappointing, and the expenses of transporting the rocks, building smelting furnaces and keeping rowdy crews on pay were bringing the company near financial collapse. According to Lok, Frobisher became so angry he "drew his dagger" against one of the assayers, a man by the name of Jonas Schutz. "He threatened to kill him if he did not finish his work out of hand, that he might set out again on the third voyage."

Schutz never did find gold in those black rocks and neither did any of the other assayers hired by the company. But the disappointing results were kept secret and by the spring of 1578 the gold fever that had gripped investors was proving unstoppable. Frobisher was authorized to lead a fleet of fifteen vessels back across the Atlantic. He was to take possession of Frislanda along the way, then sail on to Estotiland (Meta Incognita, as it was henceforth referred to in British documents), mine for gold and establish a colony of roughly one hundred men. The frame house that was to serve as the first building of the new colony was loaded aboard the *Dennis.*

Frobisher sailed off the coast of Ireland and after fourteen days reached the western coast of Greenland, which he still thought was the western coast of Frislanda. "The general and other gentlemen went ashore," Best wrote, "being the first known Christians that we have true notice of that ever set foot upon that ground." True notice? Best was probably casting doubt on the stories of old Norse colonies in the North Atlantic to ensure the legitimacy of an English claim of possession. Frobisher immediately named the land West England and went on a brief exploration of the coast "[discovering] good harbours and certain little boats of that country"—presumably kayaks. His party came upon a village, which the Inuit had hastily abandoned, "much amazed at so strange a sight [of] creatures of human shape (supposing there had been no other world but theirs), so far in apparel, complexion and other things different from themselves." The intruders looked into the tents and rummaged through the Inuit's belongings, finding among other things "a box of small nails and certain ear rings, boards of fir tree well cut, with diverse other things artificially wrought"—a great variety of artifacts which had probably once belonged to the Norse Greenlanders.

For the first time, Best expressed doubts about Frislanda's location on the Zen map, wondering whether "this West England, [which] promiseth good hope of great commodities and riches," was not in some way attached to Greenland and possibly to the coast of North America "since people, apparel and boats are so [alike]. And multitude of islands of ice does argue [in favor of] a bay which joins the two." But still, he did not question Frislanda's existence.

The fleet began the crossing toward Baffin Island but was slowed down by thick ice and fog and a pod of whales. Strong winds then scattered the fleet. The *Dennis* struck an iceberg and sunk. The crew was saved but the frame house went down with the ship. Frobisher and some of the other vessels finally reached what he took to be the entrance of the Northwest Passage (Frobisher Bay) but was in fact a large, turbulent channel that eventually led him to a vast inner sea (Hudson Bay). He called the channel Mistaken Strait and sailed west for nine days, deep into the North American continent, before retracing his route and reconnecting with the rest of the fleet at Countess of Warwick Island.

The men were quickly set to work, excavating, transporting and loading tons of black boulders in the ships' holds while the invisible Inuit watched from afar. The initial plan of establishing a mining colony— the first English colony in North America—was abandoned because the frame house had been lost at sea, together with most of the supplies for the winter. Frobisher nevertheless ordered the construction of a stone house at the top of the island, with a sweeping view of the low-lying islands scattered at the entrance of the bay. The purpose was to see how well it would survive the winter. Frobisher had it filled with a variety of objects, including mirrors and bells, which he thought might lure the Inuit and set the stage for improved relations the following year. After the ships had left, with their 1,200-ton cargo of rocks, the Inuit came ashore and picked their way through the remains of the mining operation. They demolished the house and took away the wood and nails and most of the objects Frobisher had left there for them.

Lok and his backers, meanwhile, had built in the town of Dartford, in the Thames Valley, the largest smelter in the country for the extraction of gold. As soon as the fleet arrived, the rocks were unloaded and transported overland by horse-drawn carts. But of course no matter how hard everyone tried, and how much more money was poured into the project, the rocks did not turn into gold. In the end, most of them were thrown in the Thames, though several batches were used for construction in Dartford and still today a sparkling fragment of a rock from Countess of Warwick Island is occasionally spotted in an old village wall. The whole enterprise ended in a financial fiasco of colossal proportions. Poor Lok ended up in prison, Frobisher gave up his dream of navigating the Northwest Passage all the way to Cathay and the appetite for investing in overseas exploration disappeared for a while.

Dee, however, did not give up his efforts to establish a British Empire in North America. He found a useful new ally in Richard Hakluyt, an energetic propagandist with strong imperial yearnings. In 1582, four years after Frobisher's last journey to North America, Hakluyt published *Divers Voyages Touching the Discoverie of America,* a collection of travel writings that was really a manifesto to spur England back into action. Just like Dee had done twelve years earlier, Hakluyt marveled that England had not yet found "the grace to set fast footing in such fertile and temperate places as are yet left unspoiled" by the Spaniards and the Portuguese. "I conceive great hope that the time approacheth that we of England may share and partake in parts of America."

Among the writings in his collection were those of Cartier, Verrazzano and other early explorers of North America. But the text he was especially proud to publish for the first time in English was Nicolò the Younger's book on the Zen voyages (adding, wrongly, that the papers had been collected by Ramusio). Espousing Dee's earlier view, Hakluyt concurred that "the testimony of Nicolaus and Anthonius Zeni that Estotiland is an island, doth yield no small hope" for building a British empire in North America.

It was only in 1585, seven years after the collapse of the Company of Cathay, that another great seaman, John Davis, finally sailed in Frobisher's wake. Davis was a very different kind of explorer, well educated and with a keen knowledge

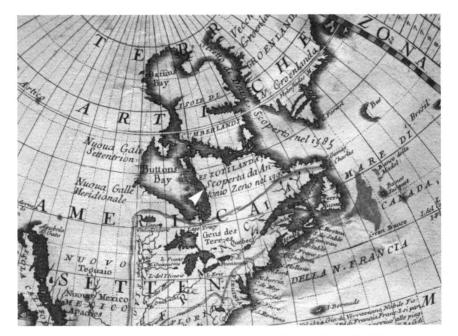

I came across this map of the New World in a friend's library in Venice. I was struck by the fact that even as late as 1688, when the map was published, Estotilanda was still very much part of the geographical landscape. The script (see arrow) reads: Estotilanda—Scoperta da Antonio Zen nel 1390 *(Estotilanda—Discovered by Antonio Zen in 1390). It was an extravagant claim to make at the end of the seventeenth century but also a testament to the enduring influence of the Zen narrative in the world of cartography.*

of geography. He landed in Greenland and identified it correctly (as Greenland, not Frislanda!). After establishing friendly relations with the Inuit, he sailed up the western coast to Disko Bay and then over to Baffin Island, across what is known today as the Davis Strait.

By then, war had broken out between Spain and England, putting another temporary stop to major expeditions across the Atlantic. But after the defeat of the Spanish Armada, the English presence in North America expanded rapidly throughout the early decades of the seventeenth century. As the coastal regions came into focus, the charts ceased to be a matter of conjecture and became increasingly accurate. The Zen map no longer had any practical use for mariners sailing west. So I was surprised to find that it continued to influence the cartography of the North Atlantic during the seventeenth century.

Of all the Zenian islands, mythical Icaria was the first to disappear from the major maps. Then it was Drogio's turn to fade away as other names replaced it along the coast of New England. Frislanda, on the other hand, stuck around for another hundred years; cartographers moved her about like a piece of old furniture one no longer has any use for but one is loath to throw away. It disappeared during the last decades of the seventeenth century, but it suddenly bobbed back to the surface on a 1701 map, off the coast of southern Greenland. Most remarkable of all was the longevity of Estotiland, a name that remained emblazoned across maps of Eastern Canada even into the eighteenth century. My own favorite was one by Vincenzo Coronelli, a Venetian mapmaker: ESTOTILANDA covered a large swath of land which included Labrador and Baffin Island, and under the finely drawn capital letters, it said: "Scoperta da Antonio Zen"— "Discovered by Antonio Zen," which was a bit of a stretch.

CHAPTER NINE

Venetian Puzzle

*Mr Konochie**
Secretary to the Royal Geographical Society
21 Regent Street 18 January 1832

Dear Sir,
I have the honour to acknowledge the reception of
your communication of my having been elected a
foreign member of the Royal Geographical Society of
London.
I request you, Sir, to express to the Royal Society in
my name how much I feel myself honoured by the
distinction and how eager I shall be to size [sic] *any*
opportunity which might present itself to contribute my
share to the attainment of those noble scientific tasks
which the society proposes to fulfil . . .
Your obedient servant,
Cpt. Christian Zahrtmann
Hydrographical Office
Copenhagen

I WAS passing through London on one of my Zen pilgrim-
ages to the north and I made a stop at the archives of the
Royal Geographical Society—that hallowed temple of
the Victorian Age. There I found this letter by Captain

---

* The first secretary of the Royal Geographical Society, Alexander
Maconochie.

Christian Zahrtmann, a Danish admiral and geographer who played a central role in the controversial history of the Zen voyages.

True to his word, Captain Zahrtmann did not wait long before contributing his share, as he put it in his letter of acknowledgment. Maconochie received in the mail an English translation of some "remarks" Zahrtmann had delivered in Copenhagen and that he now urged the board members of the RGS to publish at the earliest opportunity in the society's journal. To Maconochie's astonishment, the "remarks" turned out to be a scathing attack against the Zen voyages and the integrity of Nicolò the Younger.

Zahrtmann was not the first to raise questions about the reliability of the Zen narrative. Scholars and amateurs had debated the issue for nearly three centuries—the eighteenth-century English antiquarian John Pinkerton called Nicolò the Younger's book "one of the most puzzling in the whole circle of literature." But no one had yet accused the author of being an out-and-out liar. Zahrtmann, on the other hand, asserted Nicolò the Younger "reared his fabulous structure" by stringing together nothing but a series of "fabrications." He noted angrily "[how] difficult [it was] to select one passage in preference to another for refutation, the whole being a tissue of fiction." The vivid details about enterprising monks using hot springs for heating and cooking and growing vegetables, he said, were "not worth a refutation." He scoffed at the notion that the Zens might have joined up with the earl of Orkney to explore the old Norse dominions. If they ever did sail to the North Atlantic in the fourteenth century, he wrote dismissively, they probably joined the Vitalian Freebooters, an infamous band of marauders that in those days terrorized the coasts of the Faroes, Iceland and even Greenland.

"It is not from the south," Zahrtmann quipped unpleasantly, "that we can expect elucidations on the older north."

. . .

I WONDERED what could possibly have gotten into Zahrtmann that he should display such raw animosity toward a
Venetian nobleman who had been dead for nearly three hundred years. True, reactions to the story of the Zen brothers
tended to be extreme, the field divided between staunch sup-
porters and dedicated denigrators. But in this case the abu-
sive tone toward Nicolò the Younger seemed entirely out of
character.

Zahrtmann was a first-class geographer with a number of
ground-breaking maps to his credit, and that alone would
have been reason enough to welcome him as a member of the
Royal Geographical Society. But his induction was also an
overdue gesture of courtesy toward a man who had worked
ceaselessly to improve the safety of navigation in the North
Sea. As head of the Hydrographical Office in Copenhagen
and, from 1826 onward, as the director of the Archives of
Danish Maritime Maps, he provided a steady flow of new
charts and data to the British Admiralty at a time when free
access to the Baltic Sea was a key component of British foreign policy. Ironically, Zahrtmann had fought against the
British as a young Danish officer during the Napoleonic
Wars. But he believed very strongly that reliable nautical
information should be available to all, including former enemies, and he acted upon this principle even if it often put him
at odds with his colleagues at the Danish Admiralty.

However, after a little more digging on my part, I discovered Zahrtmann had a fiercely nationalistic side as well. He
belonged to a new generation of Danish geographers who
had been influenced by Carl Christian Rafn's groundbreak-
ing work on the Viking voyages to America and were reconnecting with their Norse heritage and the history of the early
colonization of the North Atlantic. Zahrtmann himself had
launched an ambitious mapping expedition to Greenland,
led by his close friend Captain Augustus Graah. In Copenhagen, the question of who had discovered what and when
was becoming increasingly relevant. Zahrtmann and his
friends had little patience with the notion that two Venetian

brothers had been poking around Norse territory in the fourteenth century, in the company of a Scottish laird to boot!

Yet the story of the Zen voyages was enjoying a strong revival. John Reinhold Forster, the Scots-Prussian naturalist, had been the first to reignite the debate as early as 1784 with his *History of the Voyages and Discoveries Made in the North*. Eight years later a prominent Danish geographer, Heinrich Peter von Eggers, had underscored the importance of the Zen narrative in a speech in Copenhagen of all places. And in 1808, Placido Zurla published *Dissertazione intorno ai viaggi e scoperte settentrionali di Nicolò ed Antonio fratelli Zeni*, a widely read essay on the journeys and discoveries of Messer Nicolò and Antonio. Zurla, a Venetian, was of course partial to the Zens. But as the editors of *The London Journal* summed up in the early 1830s, "The great majority of geographers have admitted the reality of the voyages of the Zeni and the general truth of the relation."

There remained one person whose immense prestige could still tip the balance the other way. But in early 1835 Alexander von Humboldt, the most influential naturalist and geographer of his time, announced he had "reviewed with impartiality" the narrative of the Zen brothers and had found in it "a candour and detailed descriptions of objects about which nothing in Europe could have given them an idea . . . and which remove all suspicion of imposture." He also pointed out that "the extreme confusion in the data . . . seems to confirm the sloppiness of the writing and the sorry state of the original manuscripts."

The favorable consensus that was building up around the Zen voyages cannot have pleased Captain Zahrtmann. But I suspect there was something more than mere national pride behind his attack against Nicolò the Younger. In the 1830s, the memory of Lord Nelson bombing Copenhagen and then capturing the entire Danish fleet during the Napoleonic Wars was still very vivid (Zahrtmann himself had participated as a young officer in the defense of the city). Denmark

had emerged from the Congress of Vienna in 1815 humili-
ated and much reduced in size. It had lost Norway to Swe-
den and had barely managed to hold on to Greenland,
Iceland and the Faroes—its old sea dominions. And across
the North Sea, it now faced the most powerful nation in the
world.

Plans for a British takeover of Iceland had been discussed
at length during the war—Sir Joseph Banks, the influential
president of the Royal Society, who had traveled to Labrador
as a young man before sailing to the Pacific with James
Cook, was the principal supporter of a British annexation of
Iceland. In truth, those plans had been more or less shelved
by the 1830s, but the Danish government remained very sensitive about British assertiveness in the North Atlantic. And
it is possible that Zahrtmann's animosity toward Nicolò the
Younger was stoked in part by geopolitical concerns. After
all, Britain had made use of the Zen voyages once before to
make imperial claims in a region the Danes considered their
backyard.

ZAHRTMANN'S ARGUMENTS turned out to be rather weak
despite his superior tone. He made, essentially, two points.
First: the Danish expedition to Greenland (1828–31) had
established that there never existed an island of Frislanda.
Second: Captain Graah had tried to explore the eastern coast
of Greenland but had found it so inhospitable that Nicolò
Zen could not possibly have visited a monastery there.

The mapping of the North Atlantic had made such considerable progress in the eighteenth and early nineteenth
centuries that Zahrtmann's insistence, at such a late date, that
"there never existed an island of Frislanda" was nothing
short of pusillanimous. The point had already been made by
others, most notably by Buache and Eggers, who had concluded that Frislanda was the Faroese archipelago (a conclusion that, incidentally, Zahrtmann agreed with!). It was also
strange that he should single out the improbability of finding

a monastery on the eastern coast of Greenland, without wondering whether it might not have been a mistake on the part of Nicolò the Younger. As Humboldt had already observed, "This monastery, heated by running hot water, where the gardens were free of ice and snow because of warm subterranean springs, seems to belong to Iceland, which abounds in thermal waters, rather than Greenland."

After some foot dragging, the Royal Geographical Society board decided that in light of Zahrtmann's fame and impeccable credentials it would go ahead and publish his paper, which appeared in the society's journal in the spring of 1835.

In the age of rising empires, geography was again, much like it had been during the Renaissance, a very popular field. The impact of Zahrtmann's essay was considerable, and not just in the rarefied world of scholars. The editors of *The North American Review,* one of the most influential literary magazines of the time, declared the Zen voyages had suffered a drubbing at the hands of a "most formidable assailant." They praised "the effort from the pen of so profound a scholar" but made the point that the attack was not without weaknesses. And this, they said, left "a ray of hope for the sanguine admirers of Venetian prowess."

The stage was set for a battle royal among champion geographers. But who was going to pick up the gauntlet? Zahrtmann's prestige was such—he was, after all, one of the most celebrated hydrographers in Europe—that it was not until four decades later that a challenger finally stepped into the ring and announced, with typical Victorian bombast, that "the ray of hope" mentioned by the editors of *The North American Review* "has expanded into noon day light."

RICHARD HENRY MAJOR is a forgotten figure today, but in the heyday of the Victorian Age he was regarded as one of Britain's top geographers. An orphan at the age of three, he was a largely self-educated man with a passion for cartography and the history of travel and discoveries. At twenty-six he gave up his job as a clerk in a Spanish mercantile house and joined the British Museum Library as the assistant to the principal librarian. He quickly rose through the ranks of the geographical establishment, obtaining important assignments at the Hakluyt Society and the Royal Geographical Society and was appointed the first keeper of the maps at the BML.

His essay on the Zen voyages was to be his last work in a long career that included major studies on Christopher Columbus and Prince Henry of Portugal. It was also the one that brought him the greatest recognition and personal satisfaction.

Major had long been intrigued by "the peculiar phenomenon of a most true and authentic narrative having been the subject of so much discredit as to have been finally condemned as a tissue of fiction." He felt it was "[his] duty" as an editor at the Hakluyt Society "to track the causes of such misconception and to free the document of discredit."

To do so he turned Zahrtmann's argument on its head: the fallacies in the narrative were not an indication of forgery, he wrote, but evidence of the text's authenticity and the author's good faith. He dwelt on errors and mistakes, he said, "because I claim the argument, advanced here for the first time, [that they are a] demonstration of the truth of the original document."

Major was convinced Nicolò the Younger was an honest man, if something of a muddler. He found "good geography in advance of its period side by side with the most preposterous blunders . . . The good part was in the fourteenth century, gathered by the ear on the spot, the bad was the sixteenth century, unapprehended from the ancient narrative." It was up to professional geographers like himself to separate the wheat from the chaff. "Ignorance of the geography of the north cannot be looked upon as a reproach to [Nicolò the Younger]."

Unwilling to wait for the reviews of his peers, Major

delivered his own verdict of the match: "The result has been to prove Admiral Zahrtmann wrong on every point and to convict him of throwing upon an honourable man, occupying no less distinguished a post as that of the Council of Ten, a series of aspersions of the most ungenerous kind."

Respectability was important to Major—in this he was rather typical of the Victorian establishment. And this included an unquestioned respect for the upper classes. Casting "aspersions" on a member of the nobility, albeit a Venetian noble living in the Renaissance, was simply not done. Fortunately, he had cleansed Nicolò the Younger's name: "The honour of a distinguished man, whose only fault as regards this ancient story was that he did not possess the geographical knowledge of today and indulged in the glowing fancies and dictions of his sunny country, has been vindicated."

Tony Campbell, the author of a biographical study on Major and an eminent geographer himself—for many years he headed the maps department at the British Library—told me when I met him in London that Major's fascination with the story of the Zens probably stemmed from his deeper interest in the Norse discovery of America. It was easy enough to agree with him—in a way I felt my own obsession with the Zens had a lot to do with the way their story had opened up the Norse world to me. But I also felt that Major had developed a warm and genuine sympathy for Nicolò the Younger and his "glowing fancies."

MAJOR NEVER traveled to Venice. Everything he knew about the Zen family he owed to an Englishman who spent much of his life sifting through dusty old documents in the Venetian archives—the last in the long and eclectic list of characters I came across in my rambling quest.

Rawdon Brown, tall and slim, his face framed by short silvery hair and a neatly cropped beard, was a very familiar figure in Venice during the middle decades of the nineteenth century—certainly the best-known English resident in town. He lived in a palazzo on the Grand Canal,* and when he was not "grubbing in the archives" or rowing Venetian style in the lagoon, he played host to prominent English tourists, regaling them with his anecdotes about Venetian history. John Ruskin's wife, Effie, observed after being chaperoned by him around the city, "The curious Mr. Brown continually talks of people who, living four or five hundred years ago, seem to have been his particular friends or guests."

When Major wrote to Brown asking him to help him with the Venetian side of the story, Brown took to the task with gusto. Indeed Major must have felt the Zens were very much among Brown's "particular friends," given the wealth of detailed information he provided in his copious letters: birth and death records, property titles, shipping leases and official notices of political appointments—all of which allowed Major to reconstruct the world of the Zens while working at his desk at the British Library.

THE VOYAGES *of the Venetian Brothers, Nicolò and Antonio Zeno, to the Northern Seas in the XIVth Century* finally appeared in 1873. With Pinkerton obviously in mind, Major stated in triumph, "The book which had been declared one of the most puzzling in the whole circle of literature will henceforth be no puzzle at all." Zahrtmann had died twenty years earlier and Major had the stage to himself. King Victor Emmanuel II of Italy made him a knight commander of the Order of the Crown of Italy for his spirited defense of the Zens—a recognition Major was so proud of that he incorporated the insignia in his own coat of arms, with its motto *Deus anchora major*—God is the greatest anchor.

To mark the event, the Hakluyt Society published an elegant, dark blue morocco–bound edition of Major's essay, with an English translation of the original narrative and up-

---

* Palazzo Dario at first, then Ca' Ferro, Palazzo Businello and finally Palazzo Gussoni Grimani della Vida.

*Palazzo Zen as it stands today on Fondamenta Santa
Caterina. The plaque honoring the Zen brothers is visible
on the far right corner of the facade.*

to-date charts of the North Atlantic. Major sent an inscribed
copy to Rawdon Brown, who bequeathed it to the Biblioteca Marciana—a gift that in the eyes of these two elderly
Victorians with white beards no doubt represented a right-
ful act of restitution from a great naval power to its glorious
predecessor.

Postscript

R H. MAJOR's celebration was premature. His essay
too was challenged and the debate over the story of
the Zen brothers has never really ceased. In 1898
a punctilious schoolteacher by the name of Frederick W.
Lucas made a comprehensive review of all the evidence and
concluded that Nicolò the Younger had perpetrated "a contemptible literary fraud—one of the most successful and
obnoxious on record." Soon the story came under attack in
Italy as well. In 1933, Andrea Da Mosto, a Venetian historian
no less, announced he had found documents showing
Messer Nicolò was in Venice at the time of his alleged shipwreck in Frislanda. Four years later, the Italian geographer
Roberto Almagià declared in the *Enciclopedia italiana* that
the Zen chart was "a fake" and the narrative "a figment of the
author's imagination." However, I must add as a cautionary
word that in Fascist Italy nothing was allowed to obscure
the fame of the nation's champion transatlantic navigator,
Christopher Columbus. After the war, in 1949, an American
geologist, William Herbert Hobbs, threw an unexpected
lifeline to the Venetian navigators: he said his own study of
the map, which took account of compass variation, "conclusively proves the Zens to have been honest and reliable
explorers far in advance of their age." In 1974, as I've already
mentioned, the amateur historian Frederick Pohl claimed to
have proof that Henry Sinclair and Antonio Zen colonized

Nova Scotia. A decade later, Giorgio Padoan, a specialist in Renaissance studies at Ca' Foscari University, went back into the archives to discover that Da Mosto's conclusions of 1933 were wrong: Messer Nicolò was *not* in Venice at the time of the landing in Frislanda after all. Furthermore, he claimed that his philological study of the text had enabled him to recognize the parts in the narrative that were clearly medieval, and therefore could be ascribed to Messer Nicolò or to Antonio, and those that had been added by Nicolò the Younger. Padoan knew how to separate the wheat from the chaff, as R. H. Major would have said. But by the time his essay was published, in 1988, the debate had long been relegated to the fringes of geographical discourse, and few people read it.

Today the vast majority of geographers and historians generally assume the story is apocryphal, especially in northern European countries, where the mere mention of the Zen brothers can still provoke an irritated twitching of the brow. To me the map and the story are still as intriguing as they were when I first stumbled upon them by chance at the Biblioteca Marciana. As the reader knows by now, I am inclined to believe that Nicolò the Younger was a first-class muddler, not a fablemonger, and that the story he tells of his forefathers offers fascinating glimpses into the past. Unlike R. H. Major, though, I suspect the book will remain "one of the most puzzling in the whole circle of literature."

MY OWN QUEST came to an end, or at least came full circle, when the following e-mail unexpectedly popped up on my computer screen one day:

Dear Mr. di Robilant,
I hear you are writing a book on the Zens. I went to Italy in 2001. I stopped by the library on Saint Mark's Square to ask about the Zens' home in Venice. Some person helped me and after half an hour found the

*location and I went to have my picture taken. He had
not heard of the Zen travels and he did not believe in
the story.*
　Tom Paul
　Madison, CT

　Mr. Paul had learned that I was writing a book about the
Zens from Niven Sinclair, but he did not know that I was the
person who had helped him out that day in the library. A
few months after receiving his e-mail I was visiting some
colleges on the East Coast with my oldest son and I arranged
to meet him at a diner in a town in Connecticut. I was surprised he seemed so familiar—our encounter years earlier
had been so brief. We sat for lunch and he showed me a pho-
tograph of himself in front of the Palazzo Zen near the
Frari. I told him how sorry I was that I had sent him to the
"wrong" palazzo, but he didn't seem to mind. "So tell me,"
he said cheerfully, "how did you come to write a book about
the Zen brothers?"

Acknowledgments

MY QUEST for the Zen brothers began in the Biblioteca Marciana in Venice, where Piero Falchetta, Tiziana Plebani and Maria Grazia Degenhardt generously gave me their time. Around the corner, at the Biblioteca Civica Correr, Piero Lucchi and Camillo Tonini helped me untangle a few knots in the tale. And Claudia Salmini offered precious guidance in the labyrinthine Archivio di Stato at the Frari. Other Venetian friends helped along the way: Donata Grimani, Girolamo Marcello, Nicolò Zen and most of all Pamela Berry. Massimo Donattini, at the University of Bologna, provided me with a useful bibliography on the Zen family early on in my research. The brave Laura Zolo, who sailed her thirty-foot sloop *7 Roses* in the wake of the Zen brothers across the Atlantic, turned out to be a great source of inspiration when I visited her in Elba.

In London, Niven Sinclair gave me enthusiastic support and voluminous material on the Sinclair family. I also received encouragement from a band of happy geographers: Catherine Delano-Smith, Tony Campbell, Peter Barber at the British Library and Francis Herbert at the Royal Geographical Society.

In Orkney, Kath Gourley, Tom Muir and Willie Thomson enlightened me on the history of their beloved islands. After his initial reticence, Brian Smith, head of the Shetland Archives in Lerwick, assisted me generously. Jonathan and Leslie Wills welcomed me warmly in Bressay. Further north, in the Faroes, Magni Arge, Jóannes Patursson, Arne Thorsteinsson and Andras Mortensen provided good company

Acknowledgments

and some illuminating insights into Faroese history as well as a few glimpses of the islands' prospects. Iceland's ambassador to Rome, Guðni Bragason, was kind enough to provide me with a translation of Jógvan Isaksen's *Adventus Domini*. In Iceland, Margaret Blondal, Arna Antonsdóttir, Steinunn Kristjánsdóttir, Olafur Asgeirsson, Þóður Tomasson, Martina Potzsch and Villi Eyjolsson were especially generous with their time.

Silvia Cosimini expertly translated some Icelandic texts for me. Father Edward Booth and Nicola Lugosch assisted me with a translation of *Thorlak's Saga*. Michele Melega read Danish material on Admiral Christian Zahrtmann for me.

Before leaving for Greenland, I benefited from the insights of Kirsten Seaver, author of *A Frozen Echo*. Several people assisted me kindly during my visit: Silverio "Silver" Scivoli, Inga Dora Markussen, Daniel Thorleifsen, Hans Lange, Jens Larsen, Christian Hansen. Most of all I would like to thank my friend Robin Navrozov for her decisive impulse before the last leg of my journey. The Greenland chapter is dedicated to her.

Notes

Prologue

6   "a tissue of fiction": Christian Zahrtmann, "Remarks on the Voyages to the Northern Hemisphere ascribed to the Zeni of Venice," *The Journal of the Royal Geographical Society* 5 (1835), p. 109.

6   "one of the most successful and obnoxious": Frederick Lucas, *The Annals of the Voyages of the Brothers Nicolò and Antonio Zeno in the North Atlantic about the End of the Fourteenth Century and the Claim founded thereon to a Venetian Discovery of America* (London: Stevens, Son and Stiles,1898), p. 143.

7   "to be filled with candor": Alexander von Humboldt, *Examen critique de l'histoire de la géographie du nouveau continent*, vol. 2 (Paris: Gide, 1836–37), p. 122.

Chapter One: Making a Book

10   "He was not pleased with my request": From the dedication in the second edition of *Dell'origine de barbari che distrussero per tutto 'l mondo l'imperio di Roma onde hebbe principio la città di Venetia* (Venice: Marcolini, 1558).

10   "not to show it to anyone": Ibid., from the original dedication in the edition of 1557, reprinted in 1558.

10   "He had been so busy performing": Ibid., from the dedication in the 1558 edition.

11   "how truly distraught": Ibid.

12   "trickster whose inventions": Tony Wood "Confections of Zeno," *Cabinet Magazine* 18 (2005), online edition.

14   "Venetians, especially young ones": *Storia della Guerra Veneto-Turca*, unpublished manuscript. Venice: Biblioteca Marciana, mss. ital., CL VII, cod. 2053, p. 194.

14   "the infamy of all Christianity": Ibid., p. 112 verso.

14   "the Spanish soldiers who were on the Emperor's ships": Ibid.

15   "Now everyone rushes to buy property": *Dell'origine*, p. 15 verso.

15   "in houses of equal size": Ibid.

15   "the indolent and the pleasure-seeking": Ibid.

16 "whose great worth and wisdom": *Dell'origine,* dedication of 1557, reprinted in 1558 edition.

16 "with loving diligence": Daniele Barbaro, *I dieci libri di Vitruvio* (Venice: Marcolini, 1556); quoted in Ennio Concina, *L'arsenale della Repubblica di Venezia* (Milano: Electa, 1984), p. 146.

16 "lifting huge weights": Ibid., p. 150.

16 "good judgment": Ibid.

17 "soul mate": *Dell'origine,* from the 1557 dedication.

17 "appease his rage": Ibid.

19 "a creature of the great Pietro": From the dedication to Duke Ercole of Ferrara in *Libro delle sorti* (Venice: Marcolini, 1560); quoted in Scipione Casali, *Gli annali della tipografia veneziana di Francesco Marcolini* (Bologna: Gerace, 1953), p. 279.

20 "Our friend Francesco's superb structure": Ibid., quoted by Luigi Servolini in the introduction.

20 "beautiful imagery": Giorgio Vasari, *Le opere* (Firenze: Passigli, 1832–38), p. 691.

21 "not a little familiarity": *Dell'origine,* dedication of 1557 reprinted in the 1558 edition.

22 "quite inaccurate": Giovanni Battista Ramusio, *Navigazioni e viaggi,* vol. 1 (Torino: Einaudi, 1978), p. 4.

22 "I think it would be good and not a little useful": Ibid.

24 "by stealing time from Time": *Navigazioni,* vol. 1, p. 8.

24 "The Spaniards . . . tell us there are many countries": *Storia della Guerra,* p. 3.

24 "so many territories": Ibid., p. 58.

24 "the documents I have been able to salvage": Nicolò Zen, *Dello scoprimento dell'isole Frislanda, Eslanda, Engrovelanda, Estotilanda e Icaria fatto sotto il Polo Artico da due fratelli Zeni, Messer Nicolò Cavaliere e Messer Antonio* (Venice: Marcolini, 1558), p. 58.

25 "When I was a child": Ibid., p. 57.

25 "on an old and rotten chart": Ibid., p. 47.

27 "The loss has been very substantial": *Navigazioni,* vol. 3, p. 4.

28 "damaged and filled with mistakes": Ibid., vol. 1, p. 5.

28 "I hesitate a long time": Ibid.

28 "many sleepless nights": Ibid.

30 "wondrous things": *Dello scoprimento,* from the dedication to Daniel Barbaro.

Chapter Two: Messer Nicolò

31 "After the war against the Genovese": *Dello scoprimento,* p. 46.

36 "where we accosted": Daniele di Chinazzo, *Cronica de la Guerra da Veniciani a Zenovesi,* edited by Vittorio Lazzarini (Venice: Deputazione di Storia Patria per le Venezie, 1958), p. 215.

36 "We raided the ships": Ibid.

36 "the men were chopped to pieces": Ibid.

36   "a bombardment of heavy rocks": Ibid.
37   "a strong desire to fight": Ibid., p. 216.
37   "all the biscuit he could find": Ibid., p. 218.
44   "[build] and [equip] a ship with his own riches": *Dello scoprimento*, p. 46.
48   "He was caught in a fierce storm": Ibid.

Chapter Three: Frislanda

49   "Messer Nicolò landed": *Dello scoprimento*, p. 46.
49   "they were unlikely to put up": Ibid., p. 46 verso.
50   *"grandissima allegrezza"*: Ibid., p. 46.
51   "lord of Sorant": Ibid., p. 46 verso.
51   "a group of islands": Ibid.
51   "Zichmni quicky understood": Ibid., p. 47.
52   "While Zichmni led": Ibid., p. 47 verso.
52   "The sea in which": Ibid.
52   "First the rebel chiefs": Ibid.
54   "came out rather well": Ibid., p. 47.
63   "following the advice": Ibid., p. 47 verso.
63   "conquered the enemy": Ibid.

Chapter Four: Zichmni

69   "triumphantly": *Dello scoprimento*, p. 48.
69   "set in such a way as to form a great number of gulfs": Ibid.
69   "hauling copious catches": Ibid.
69   "the principal city of the island": Ibid.
70   "whose great valor and goodness": Ibid., p. 57 verso.
70   "employed on the subject": John Rheinhold Forster, *History of the Voyages and the Discoveries in the North* (London: Robinson, 1786), p. 181.
71   "far more closely resembles Wichmannus": *The Annals of the Voyages*, p. 96.
71   "ruled over Porlanda": *Dello scoprimento*, p. 46 verso.
72   "a natural corruption of [the name]": Barbara Crawford, "The Earls of Orkney-Caithness and Their Relations with Norway and Scotland 1158–1470" (PhD thesis, University of St. Andrews, 1971).
76   "up to a hundred armed men": *Diplomatarium norvegicum*, vol. 2 (Oslo: 1849–70), p. 353. Quoted in *Records of the Earldom of Orkney* (Edinburgh: Scottish History Society, 1914), p. 21.
77   "one thousand golden pieces": Ibid.
84   "tripe": Brian Smith, "The Zen Voyages," *The New Orkney Antiquarian Journal* 2 (2002).
84   "most blatant hoaxer": Ibid.
84   "middling rank": William Thomson, conversation with the author.

86 "Many ships come here to take large consignments": *Dello scoprimento*, p. 48.

86 "He purchased a ship": Ibid., p. 48 verso.

87 "greeted him with great joy": Ibid.

87 "If any may wish to attack": *Diplomatarium norvegicum*, vol. 2, p. 353.

87 "in full military regalia": *Dello scoprimento*, p. 48 verso.

90 "few and poorly armed": Ibid., p. 49.

91 "what remained of his army": Ibid.

93 "he rigged up his three ships": Ibid.

Chapter Five: Islanda

94 "The place was a wonder to behold": Ibid., p. 50.

97 "scalding water": Ibid., p. 51.

97 "they simply let in the cold": Ibid., p. 49 verso.

97 "hold them in great awe": Ibid.

98 "The dough rises": Ibid.

98 "The men go up to the crater": Ibid.

98 "The builders start with": Ibid., p. 50.

99 "a thousand other chores": Ibid.

103 "he organized the monks' life so beautifully": At the time of my trip to Iceland there were no English translations of *Thorlak's Saga* available. A rough translation was provided to me by Nicola Lugosch, then a PhD student working on a thesis on Thorlak. This particular sentence is at the end of chapter 7.

111 "Strange things are happening to me": Anonymous, *Njall's Saga* (London: Penguin Classics, 2002), p. 217.

Chapter Six: Estotiland, Drogio and Icaria

114 "Being unaccustomed to the bitter cold": *Dello scoprimento*, p. 51 verso.

115 "But despite all his efforts and prayers": Ibid.

118 "I have merely substituted": Ibid.

118 "Four fishing boats": Ibid.

122 "a very high mountain": Benedetto Bordone, *Isolario*, book 1 (Venice: Zoppino, 1534), p. xii.

123 "fairly agrees . . . a little less": Richard Henry Major, "The Site of the Lost Colony of Greenland Determined," *The Journal of the Royal Geographical Society* 43 (1873), p. 202.

125 "some twelve days away from Norway": From a letter written by Pope Alexander III to the Norwegian archbishop in Trondheim, quoted in Kirsten Seaver, *The Frozen Echo* (Stanford, Calif.: Stanford University Press, 1996), p. 34.

126 "absolutely certain": Ibid.

126 "Subject to such sophistications": "The Site of the Lost Colony," p. 202.

128 "of a country very large": *Dello scoprimento*, p. 53.

128   "Many are those": Ibid., p. 54.
128   "a bad omen": Ibid.
128   "into a sea of gloom": Ibid., p. 54 verso.
129   "battered and thrown about": Ibid.
129   "and we never knew": Ibid.
129   "great torment": Ibid.
129   "As we reached": Ibid.
129   "The man said the name": Ibid.
131   "The interpreter told us": Ibid.
131   "so they could learn": Ibid., p 55.
132   "in great hurry": Ibid., p. 55 verso.
132   "They rushed down": Ibid.
132   "A vast and well-armed multitude": Ibid.
133   "to him that found the New Isle": Samuel Eliot Morison, *The European Discovery of America: The Northern Voyages* (New York: Oxford University Press, 1971), pp. 187–88.
133   "clothed in beast skins and ate raw flesh": Richard Biddle, *A Memoir of Sebastian Cabot* (London: Hurst, Chance and Co., 1831), p. 229.
133   "The sea grew rougher": *Dello scoprimento*, p. 56.

Chapter Seven: Engroneland

136   "scruffy wimps": *The Frozen Echo*, p. 21. Kirsten Seaver writes: "*Skraelings*—a contemptuous term, loosely translatable as 'scruffy wimps,' which the Norse used to describe the natives of Greenland and North America."
139   "at the start of June": *Dello scoprimento*, p. 56 verso.
139   "The air was sweet": Ibid.
140   "We saw smoke": Ibid., p. 56.
140   "they immediately gorged": Ibid., p. 56 verso.
140   "short creatures": Ibid.
140   "pusillanimous dwarfs": *Isolario*, book 1, p. v verso.
141   "Inside was as a great fire": *Dello scoprimento*, p. 56 verso.
151   "The air was clean": Ibid.
151   "They were tired": Ibid.
152   "Against my will": Ibid., p. 57.
152   "I knew the island": Ibid.
152   "both sides of Engroviland": Ibid.
153   "I describe in it the countries": Ibid., p. 57 verso.
153   "the life and deeds": Ibid.
153   "I will add no more": Ibid.

Chapter Eight: Squaring the Circle

154   "*relicta ser Antonii Zeno*": Archivio di Stato di Venezia, Cancelleria, folder 170, notaio Marco de Raphanellis.

160 "after twenty days of high fever": Ennio Concina, *L'Arsenale della Repubblica di Venezia* (Milan: Electa, 1984), p.153.

163 "the squaring of the circle": From the memoirs of Walter Ghim, quoted in John Noble Wilford, *The Mapmakers* (New York: Vintage, 2001), p. 89.

165 "an authority universally thought": Remark by Girolamo Ruscelli, quoted in William Herbert Hobbs, "Zeno and the Cartography of Greenland," *Imago Mundi* 6 (1949), p. 17.

166 "the North part": Abraham Ortelius, *Theatrum orbis terrarum*, fol. 6, quoted in *The North American Review* 47 (1838), p. 191.

166 "the best geographer": Nicholas Crane, *Mercator* (New York: Henry Holt, 2004), p. 247.

166 "for collecting the maps": *Mercator*, p. 248.

168 "most commodious": John Dee, *Mathematical Praeface to the Elements of Geometrie of Euclid of Megara* (London: 1570).

168 "half challenged by the learned": Ibid.

168 "and little and little wynne": Ibid.

169 "It will be universally agreed": John Dee, *The Limits of the British Empire*, edited by Ken MacMillan and Jennifer Abeles (Westport, Conn.: Praeger Publishers, 2004), p. 38.

170 "rising like pinnacles of steeples": The comment is by Christopher Hall, Frobisher's navigator, and is quoted in Robert McGhee, *The Last Imaginary Place* (Oxford: Oxford University Press, 2006), p. 156.

171 "great open sea": Richard Collinson, *The Three Voyages of Martin Frobisher* (London: The Hakluyt Society, 1867), p. 83.

172 "This recovery is speedily": *The Limits of the British Empire*, p. 48.

173 "the Spaniard occupieth not": Ibid.

173 "I declared to the Queen": *The Private Diary of Dr John Dee*, edited by James Orchard Halliwell (London: Camden Society, 1842), p. 4. Entry for Nov. 28, 1577.

173 "Concerning a New Location": *The Limits of the British Empire*, p. 37.

174 "Certain Noteworthy things": Ibid., p. 38.

176 "We made the land perfect": *The Three Voyages of Martin Frobisher*, p. 124.

176 "appeareth by a description": Ibid., p. 125.

176 "[The Zens] have in their sea cards": Ibid.

177 "islands of ice": Ibid., p. 126.

177 "great bigness and depth": Ibid.

177 "fresh and sweet to the taste": Ibid.

177 "bred in the sounds": Ibid.

177 "lying becalmed": Ibid., p. 125.

177 "a great fish called a hollibut": Ibid.

177 "a kind of coral": Ibid.

177 "may be found very rich": Ibid.

177 "we plucked down our tents": Ibid., p. 152.

178 "drew his dagger": *The Last Imaginary Place*, p. 165.

178 "He threatened to kill him": Ibid.

178 "The general and other gentlemen": *The Three Voyages of Martin Frobisher*, p. 232.

178 "much amazed": Ibid., p. 233.

178 "a box of small nails": Ibid.

179 "this West England": Ibid.

180 "the grace to set fast footing": Richard Hakluyt, *Divers Voyages touching the Discoverie of America and the Islands Adjacent* (London: 1582), p. 8.

180 "I conceive great hope": Ibid., p. 23.

Chapter Nine: Venetian Puzzle

184 "one of the most puzzling": John Pinkerton, *History of Scotland*, vol. 1, p. 261n, quoted in *The Voyages of the Venetian Brothers, Nicolò and Antonio Zeno, to the Northern Seas, in the XIVth Century* (London: The Hakluyt Society, 1873), introduction, p. iii.

184 "reared his fabulous structure": Remarks on the Voyages," p. 119.

184 "fabrications": Ibid., p. 128.

184 "[how] difficult [it was] to select": Ibid., p. 109.

184 "not worth a refutation": Ibid., p. 112.

184 "It is not from the south": Ibid., p. 126.

186 "The great majority of geographers": "Voyages of the Zeni," *Leigh Hunt's London Journal*, August 15, 1835, n. 72.

186 "reviewed with impartiality": *Examen critique*, p. 122.

186 "the extreme confusion": Ibid.

187 "there never existed an island of Frislanda": "Remarks on the Voyages," p. 105.

188 "This monastery": *Examen critique*, p. 127.

188 "most formidable assailant": *The Voyages of the Venetian Brothers*, p. vii.

188 "the effort from the pen": Ibid., p. viii.

188 "a ray of hope": Ibid.

188 "has expanded into noon day light": *The Voyages of the Venetian Brothers*, p. viii.

189 "the peculiar phenomenon": Ibid., p. i.

189 "duty . . . to track": Ibid., pp. i and ii.

189 "because I claim the argument": Ibid., p. xxvi.

189 "good geography": Ibid., p. xxxvii.

189 "Ignorance of the geography of the north": Ibid., p. xxv.

190 "The result has been to prove": Ibid., p. viii.

190 "The honour of a distinguished man": Ibid., p. cii.

191 "grubbing in the archives": John Law, "Grubbing in the Archives: Rawdon Brown and Venetian Sources," in *Rawdon Brown and the Anglo-Venetian Relationship*, edited by Ralph Griffiths and John Law (Stroud, Gloucestershire: Nonsuch, 2005), p. 135.

191 "The curious Mr. Brown continually talks": *Effie in Venice,* edited by Mary Lutyens (London: Pallas Editions, 2001), p. 107.

191 "The book which had been declared": *The Voyages of the Venetian Brothers,* p. cii.

Postscript

193 "a contemptible literary fraud": *The Annals of the Voyages,* p. 143.

193 "a fake": Roberto Almagià, *Enciclopedia Italiana Treccani,* vol. 35 (Rome: 1949), p. 921.

193 "a figment of the author's imagination": Ibid.

193 "conclusively proves": "Zeno and the Cartography of Greenland," p. 19.

Select Bibliography

The Zen Controversy

The story of the Zen voyages has generated enough books and articles in the past four and a half centuries to fill a small library. The following is a list of the more significant ones:

Beauvois, Eugène. *Les voyages transatlantiques des Zeno.* Louvain: Istas, 1890.

Beazley, Raymond. "The Voyages of the Zeni." *The Geographical Journal,* 13, no.2 (1899), pp. 166–170.

Buache, Jean Nicolas. *"Mémoire sur l'île de Frislande,"* in *Histoire de l'Académie des Sciences.* Paris: 1787, pp. 430–53.

Da Mosto, Andrea. *"I navigatori Nicolò e Antonio Zen,"* in *Ad Alessandro Luzio gli Archivi di Stato Italiano. Miscellanea di studi storici,* vol. 1. Florence: Le Monnier, 1933, pp. 293–308.

Eggers, Heinrich Peter von. *Uber die Wahre Lage des alten Ostgronlands.* Kiel: 1794.

Fiske, John. *The Discovery of America.* New York: Houghton Mifflin, 1892.

Forster, John Reinhold. *History of the Voyages and Discoveries made in the North.* London: Robinson, 1786.

Hobbs, William H. "Zeno and the Cartography of Greenland." *Imago Mundi* 6 (1949): pp. 15–19.

Humboldt, Alexander von. *Examen critique de l'histoire de la géographie du nouveau continent,* 2 vols. Paris: Gide, 1836–37.

Krarup, F. *Zeniers Reise til Norden.* Copenhagen: 1878.

Lelewel, Joaquin. *"Tavola di navicare di Nicolò e Antonio Zeni."* *Geographie di Moyen Age* 4 (1852): pp. 77–108.

Lucas, Frederick W. *The Annals of the Voyages of the Brothers Nicolò and Antonio Zeno in the North Atlantic about the End of the Fourteenth Century and the Claim found thereon to a Venetian Discovery of America.* London: Stevens, Son and Stiles, 1898.

Major, Richard Henry. "The Site of the Lost Colony of Greenland Determined and Pre-Columbian Discoveries of America Confirmed, from

14th Century Documents." *The Journal of the Royal Geographical Society* 43 (1873): pp. 156–206.

——. *The Voyages of the Venetian Brothers Nicolò and Antonio Zeno in the Northern Seas in the XIV Century.* London: The Hakluyt Society, 1873.

Malte-Brun, Conrad. *Atlas complet du précis de la géographie universelle.* Paris: Aimé André, 1832.

Padoan, Giorgio. "*Sulla relazione cinquecentesca dei viaggi nord-atlantici di Nicolò e Antonio Zen (1383–1403).*" *Quaderni veneti* 9 (1989): pp. 7–104.

Pohl, Frederick J. *Prince Henry Sinclair: His Expedition to the New World in 1398.* New York: Potter, 1974.

Rafn, Carl Christian. *Antiquitates americanae, sive scriptores septentrionales rerum ante-columbianarum.* Copenhagen: Societas Regia Antiquariarum Septentrionalium, 1837.

Ramusio, Giovanni Battista. *Navigazioni e viaggi,* edited by Marica Milanesi, 6 vols. Turin: Einaudi, 1978.

Smith, Brian. "The Zen Voyages." *The New Orkney Antiquarian Journal* 2 (2002); online edition.

Steenstrup, Japetus. *Les voyages des frères Zeni dans le nord: compte rendu du Congrès des américanistes.* Copenhagen: 1884.

Storm, Gustav. *Om Zeniernes rejser.* Christiania: Norske Geografiske Selskab, 1891.

Terra Rossa, Padre Vitale. *Riflessioni geografiche circa le terre incognite.* Padua: Cadorino, 1686.

"The Voyages of the Zeni." *The North American Review* 47 (1838): pp. 177–206.

Torfeus, Thormod. *Historia Vinlandiae antiquae.* Copenhagen: 1705.

"Voyages of the Zeni." *Leigh Hunt's London Journal* 72 (1835), p. 271.

Wood, Tony. "Confections of Zeno." *Cabinet Magazine* 18 (2005); online edition.

Zahrtmann, Christian. "Remarks on the Voyages to the Northern Hemisphere Ascribed to the Zenis of Venice." *The Journal of the Royal Geographical Society* 5 (1835): pp. 102–28.

Zen, Nicolò. *De i Commentarii del viaggio in Persia di M. Caterino Zeno il K. et delle guerre fatte nell'Imperio Persiano, dal tempo di Ussuncassano in qua. Et dello scoprimento dell'isole Frislanda, Eslanda, Engroveland, Estotilanda, et Icaria, fatto sotto il Polo Artico, da due fratelli Zeni, M. Nicolò l K. et M. Antonio. Libro uno. Con un disegno particolare di tutte le dette parti di tramontana da lor scoperte.* Venice: Marcolini, 1558.

Zurla, Placido. *Dissertazione intorno ai viaggi e scoperte settentrionali di Nicolò ed Antonio fratelli Zeno.* Venice: Zerletti, 1808.

Select Bibliography

Venice in the Late Middle Ages

In the 1980s Giorgio Padoan, eminent scholar of medieval and Renaissance studies and a longtime professor at Venice's Ca' Foscari University, combed the Archivio di Stato for information on Nicolò and Antonio Zen: birth and death certificates related to their families, official appointments, property deeds, wills, etc. I made ample use of his prodigious research during my own hunt for archival material on the Zen family. Padoan's exhaustive 1989 essay (see above) contains a detailed list of documents and their classification.

The following is a short bibliography on the late-medieval world of Nicolò and Antonio Zen:

Balard, Michel. "La lotta contro Genova," in *Storia di Venezia dalle origini della Serenissima alla caduta della Repubblica,* vol. 3. Rome: Enciclopedia Treccani, 1997, pp. 87–126.

Blanc, Alberto. *Le flotte mercantili dei veneziani.* Venice: Ongania, 1896.

Carus-Wilson, Eleanora Mary. *Medieval Merchant Venturers: Collected Studies.* London: Methuen, 1954.

Cessi, Roberto. *Politica ed economia di Venezia nel Trecento.* Rome: Edizioni di Storia e Letteratura, 1952.

Chinazzo, Daniele di. *Cronica de la guerra di veneciani a zenovesi,* edited by Vittorio Lazzarini. Venice: Deputazione di Storia Patria per le Venezie, 1958.

Doumerc, Bernard. "Le galere da mercato," in *Storia di Venezia,* vol. 12, *Il mare.* Rome: Enciclopedia Treccani, 1991, pp. 357–95.

Hocquet, Jean Claude. "I meccanismi dei traffici," in *Storia di Venezia,* vol. 3. Rome: Enciclopedia Treccani, 1997, pp. 529–616.

———. "L'armamento privato," in *Storia di Venezia,* vol. 12, *Il mare.* Rome: Enciclopedia Treccani, 1991, pp. 397–434.

Lane, Frederick C. *Venice: A Maritime Republic.* Baltimore: The Johns Hopkins University Press, 1973.

———. *Andrea Barbarigo, Merchant of Venice 1418–1449.* Baltimore: The Johns Hopkins University Press, 1944.

———. *Venetian Ships and Shipbuilders of the Renaissance.* Baltimore: The Johns Hopkins University Press, 1934.

Luzzatto, Gino. *Storia economica di Venezia dall' XI al XVI secolo.* Venice: Centro Internazionale dell'Arte e del Costume, 1961.

———. *"Navigazione di linea e navigazione libera." Studi di Storia Economica Veneziana.* Padua: 1954, pp. 53–58.

Molmenti, Pompeo. *La storia di Venezia nella vita privata dalle origini alla caduta della Repubblica,* 3 vols. Bergamo: Istituto Italiano d'Arti Grafiche, 1908.

Norwich, John Julius. *A History of Venice.* New York: Knopf, 1982.

Select Bibliography

Sapori, Armando. *The Italian Merchant in the Middle Ages*. New York: Norton, 1970.

Stokly, Doris. *Le système de l'Incanto des galées du marché de Venise (fin du 13ième siècle—milieu du 15ième siècle)*. Leiden, New York, Koln: Brill, 1995.

Tenenti, Alberto, and Corrado Vivanti. *"Le film d'un grand système de navigation: les galere marchandes vénitiennes (XV-XVI siècles)."* Annales d'economie, société et civilisation 16, no. 1 (1961): pp. 83–86.

Tucci, Ugo. *"L'impresa marittima: uomini e mezzi,"* in Storia di Venezia, vol. 2. Rome: Enciclopedia Treccani, 1995, pp. 627–59.

Zen, Jacopo. *Vita Caroli Zeni*. Bologna: Zanichelli, 1940–41.

On the Renaissance World of Nicolò the Younger

Barbaro, Daniele. *I dieci libri del'architettura di Vitruvio*. Venice: Marcolini, 1556.

Bordone, Benedetto. *Isolario*. Venice: Zoppino, 1534.

Broc, Numa. *La geografia del Rinascimento*. Modena: Panini, 1996.

Casali, Scipione. *Gli annali della tipografia veneziana di Francesco Marcolini*. Bologna: Gerace, 1953. Reprint of the 1861 edition, with an introduction by Luigi Servolini.

Concina, Ennio. *Dell'Arabico: a Venezia tra Rinascimento e Oriente*. Venice: Marsilio, 1990.

———. *"Fra Oriente ed Occidente: gli Zen, un palazzo e il mito di Trebizonda,"* in Tafuri, Manfredo, *Renovatio Urbis: Venezia nell'età di Andrea Gritti*. Rome: Officina Edizioni, 1986.

———. *L'Arsenale della Repubblica di Venezia*. Milan: Electa, 1984.

Cozzi, Gaetano. *Repubblica di Venezia e Stati Italiani*. Torino: Einaudi, 1882.

Crouzet-Pavan, Elizabeth. *Venezia trionfante: gli orizzonti di un mito*. Torino: Einaudi, 2001.

Epstein, Marion. *Francesco Marcolini, Anton Francesco Doni and Pietro Aretino: Facts, Figures and Fancies*. Unpublished manuscript, 1979. Venice: Biblioteca Marciana.

Frommel, Sabine. *"Sebastiano Serlio e il palazzo Zen a Venezia."* Annali di architettura 13 (2001): pp. 53–69.

———. *Sebastiano Serlio architetto*. Milano: Electa, 1997.

Magnus, Olaus. *Historia de gentibus septentrionalibus*. Rome: 1555.

Penrose, Boies. *Travel and Discovery in the Renaissance, 1420–1620*. Cambridge, Mass.: Harvard University Press, 1952.

Procaccioli, Paolo, ed., *Studi per "Le Sorti": Gioco, immagini, poesia oracolare a Venezia nel Cinquecento*. Treviso-Roma: Fondazione Benetton Studi e Ricerche—Viella, 2007.

Procaccioli, Paolo, and Angelo Romano, eds. *Cinquecento capriccioso e irregolare: Eresie letterarie nell'Italia del classicismo.* Manziana: Vecchiarelli, 1999.

Quondam, Amedeo. *"Nel giardino del Marcolini: un editore veneziano tra Aretino e Doni,"* Giornale storico della letteratura italiana 97 (1980): pp. 75–116.

———. *"La letteratura in tipografia." Letteratura italiana,* vol. 2. Torino: Einaudi, 1983, pp. 555–686.

Richardson, Brian. *Print Culture in Renaissance Italy.* Cambridge: Cambridge University Press, 1994.

Sansovino, Francesco. *Venetia città nobilissima et singolare descritta in XIII libri.* Venice: Martinioni, 1663.

Saxl, Fritz. *"Veritas filia temporis,"* in *Philosophy and History: Essays Presented to Ernst Cassirer.* Oxford: Oxford University Press, 1936, pp. 197–222.

Tafuri, Manfredo. *Venezia e il Rinascimento.* Torino: Einaudi,1985.

———. *Renovatio Urbis: Venezia nell'età di Andrea Gritti 1523–1538.* Rome: Officina Edizioni, 1984.

Vaccaro, Emerenziano. *Le marche dei tipografi.* Florence: Olschki, 1983.

Vasari, Giorgio. *Le opere.* Firenze: Passigli, 1832–38.

Zappella, Giuseppina. *Le marche dei tipografi e degli editori italiani del Cinquecento.* Editrice Bibliografica, 1986.

Zen, Nicolò. *Storia della Guerra Veneto-Turca.* Unpublished manuscript. Venice: Biblioteca Marciana.

———. *Dell'origine de barbari che distrussero per tutto 'l mondo l'imperio di Roma onde hebbe principio la città di Venetia.* Venice: Marcolini, 1558.

Zorzi, Renzo. *L'epopea delle scoperte.* Florence: Fondazione Giorgio Cini, 1994. See in particular Liberatori Prati, Elisa Vittoria, "Nuove ricerche su Cristoforo Colombo nella Venezia del tardo Cinquecento: le historie di don Fernando," pp. 135–61.

The Zen Voyages in Relation to Renaissance Cartography

Andrews, Kenneth. *Trade, Plunder and Settlement: Maritime Enterprise and the Genesis of the British Empire 1480–1630.* Cambridge: Cambridge University Press, 1984.

Armitage, David. *Ideological Origins of the British Empire.* Cambridge: Cambridge University Press, 2000.

Barrow, John. *A Chronological History of Voyages to the Arctic Regions.* London: John Murray, 1818.

Collinson, Richard. *The Three Voyages of Martin Frobisher.* London: The Hakluyt Society, 1867.

Select Bibliography

Crane, Nicholas. *Mercator: The Man Who Mapped the World.* New York: Henry Holt, 2003.

Fenton, Edward. *The Diaries of John Dee.* Oxfordshire: Day Books, 1998.

Hakluyt, Richard. *Divers Voyages touching the Discovery of America and the islands adjacent.* London: 1682.

Karrow, Robert W. *Map Makers of the Sixteenth Century and Their Maps.* Chicago: Speculum Orbis Press, 1993.

Kohl, Johann G. *A Documentary History of the State of Maine.* Vol. 1, *A History of the Discovery of the East Coast of North America.* Portland: Maine Historical Society, 1869.

Lambert, Andrew. "This Is All We Want: Great Britain and the Baltic Approaches 1815–1914," in *Britain and Denmark: Political, Economic and Cultural Relations in the 19th and 20th Centuries,* edited by Jørgen Sevaldsen, Claus Bjørn and Bo Bjørke. Copenhagen: Museum Tusculanum Press, 2002, pp. 147–69.

MacMillan, Ken. *Sovereignty and Possession in the English New World: The Legal Foundation of Empire 1576–1640.* Cambridge: Cambridge University Press, 2004.

MacMillan, Ken, with Jennifer Abeles. *John Dee: The Limits of the British Empire.* Westport, Conn.: Praeger, 2004.

McDermott, James. *Martin Frobisher, Elizabethan Privateer.* New Haven and London: Yale University Press, 2001.

McGhee, Robert. *The Last Imaginary Place: A Human History of the Arctic World.* Oxford: Oxford University Press, 2006.

——. *The Arctic Voyages of Martin Frobisher: An Elizabethan Adventure.* Montreal and Kingston: McGill-Queen's University Press, 2001.

Morison, Samuel Eliot. *The European Discovery of America: The Northern Voyages, A.D. 500- 1600.* Oxford: Oxford University Press, 1971.

Ortelius, Abraham. *Theatrum orbis terrarum.* Antwerp: 1570.

Roberts, Julian, and Andrew Watson, eds. *John Dee's Library Catalogue.* London: Bibliographical Society, 1990.

Wallis, Helen. "England's Search for the Northern Passage in the 16th and Early 17th centuries." *Arctic* 37, no. 4 (1984): pp. 463–72.

Wilford, John Noble. *The Mapmakers.* New York: Random House, 1981.

On the Zen Trail

Before starting out I read Laura Zolo's account of her sailing trip across the North Atlantic (*Oltre l'orizzonte: la rotta di "7 Roses" sulla scia dei fratelli Zeno.* Rome: Editrice Incontri Nautici, 2003). Along the way I found the following books were useful to me; this collection of titles came together rather casually during my journey and is in no way meant to be a comprehensive list.

Select Bibliography

Orkney and Shetland

Anderson, Peter. *Black Patie: The Life and Times of Patrick Stewart, Earl of Orkney, Lord of Shetland.* Edinburgh: John Donald Publishers, 1992.

Anonymous. *Orkneyinga Saga: The History of the Earls of Orkney,* translated by Hermann Palsson and Paul Edwards. London: Penguin Classics, 1981.

Clouston, Joseph S., ed. *Records of the Earldom of Orkney 1299–1614.* Edinburgh: Constable, 1914.

Crawford, Barbara. "The Earls of Orkney-Caithness and Their Relations with Norway and Scotland, 1158–1470." PhD dissertation, Saint Andrew's University, 1971.

Jakobsen, Jakob. *The Place Names of Shetland.* Orkney: The Orcadian Ltd., 1993, reprint of the 1936 edition.

Mackay Brown, George. *Vinland.* London: John Murray, 1992.

Saint-Clair, Roland William. *The Saint Clair of the Isles.* Auckland: Brett, 1898.

Smith, Hance. *Shetland, Life and Trade 1550–1914.* Edinburgh: John Donald Publishers, 1984.

Thomson, William. *The New History of Orkney.* Edinburgh: Mercat Press, 2001.

Faroe Islands

Anonymous. *The Tale of Thrond of Gate commonly called Faereyinga Saga,* translated by Frederick York Powell. London: Nutt, 1896.

Isaksen, Jógvan. *Adventus Domini.* Tórshavn: Mentunargrunnur Studentafelagsins, 2007.

West, John. *Faroe: The Emergence of a Nation.* London: Christopher & Co., 1972.

Wylie, Jonathan. *The Faroe Islands.* Kentucky: Kentucky University Press, 1987.

Iceland

Agnarsdóttir, Anna. *Great Britain and Iceland 1800–1820.* PhD dissertation, London School of Economics and Political Science, 1989.

Anonymous. *Njal's Saga,* translated by Leifur Eiriksson with an introduction by Robert Cook. London: Penguin Classics, 2001.

——. *The Sagas of Icelanders,* edited by Ornolfur Thorsson. London: Penguin Books, 2001.

——. *Thorlak's Saga.* Manuscript translated by Nicola Lugosch.

Select Bibliography

Byoch, Jesse L. *Medieval Iceland: Society, Sagas & Power.* Berkeley: University of California Press, 1988.

Gjerset, Knut. *History of Iceland.* London: Allen & Unwin, 1924.

Jochens, Jenny. "The Church and Sexuality in Medieval Iceland." *Journal of Medieval History* 6 (1980): pp. 377–92.

Johanneson, Jon. *A History of the Old Icelandic Commonwealth.* Winnipeg: University of Manitoba Press, 1974.

Karlsson, Gunnar. *Iceland's 1100 Years: History of a Marginal Society.* London: Hurst & Company, 2000.

Magnusson, Magnus. *The Viking Expansion Westward.* London: Bodley Head, 1973.

Greenland

Anonymous. *The Vinland Sagas: The Norse Discovery of America,* translated by Magnus Magnusson and Hermann Palsson. London: Penguin Classics, 2003.

Gad, Finn. *The History of Greenland.* London: Hurst & Company, 1970.

Jones, Gwyn. *The Norse Atlantic Saga.* Oxford: Oxford University Press, 1986.

Jones, Gwyn, ed. and trans. *Eirik the Red and Other Icelandic Sagas.* Oxford: Oxford University Press, 1961.

Seaver, Kirsten. *The Frozen Echo: Greenland and the Exploration of North America circa A.D. 1000–1500.* Stanford, Calif.: Stanford University Press, 1996.

Smiley, Jane. *The Greenlanders.* New York: Knopf, 1988.

Index

Page numbers in *italics* refer to illustrations and maps.

Index

Index

Index

Index

Index

Index

Index

and pride in Venice, 115
and publication of Zen narrative,
29, 159
recounting of fisherman's tale by,
118–24, 126–8
rift between Marcolini and,
10–12, 17, 21
on Zen voyage, 44, 50, 51–2, 97–9
see also Zen map; Zen narrative
(*Dello scoprimento*...)
Zen, Ottaviano, 157
Zen, Pietro (Dragone, the Dragon,
son of Antonio), 116, 153,
155–6
Zen, Pietro (grandfather of Nicolò
the Younger), 13, 15, 19
Zen, Pietro (great-grandson of
Antonio), 157, 158
Zen, Pietro (the Dragon, father of
Messer Nicolò), 33, 155
Zen, Raniero, 33
Zen, Tommaso, 34, 39, 116, 154,
155
Zen, Vincenzo (brother of Nicolò
the Younger), 157
Zen, Vincenzo (uncle of Nicolò the
Younger), 156, 157
Zen crest, 13
Zen family, 17, 20, 32–3
confusion of names within, 32
as merchants, 15, 155–6, 157
Zeni, Nicolaus and Anthonius, 181
Zen map, 2, 5–6, 25, 28, 50, 53,
54–55, 62, 67, 69, 72, 73*n*, 88,
89, 95, 100, *115*, 123, 127, 128,
130, *137*, 152, 160–2, 170–1,
176, 179, 182, *230*
used by Mercator, 6, 160–1, *164*,
165–6
Zen narrative (*Dello scoprimento*...)
(Nicolò the Younger), 2, 4–5,

28–30, 31, 61, 62, 66, 70, 72,
159, *161*, 165, 181, *181*, 191–2
in *Adventus Domini*, 67–8
apologists for, 78–80, 186,
188–94
author's initial interest in, 3–9
Dee's use of, 173–4
discredited as forgery, 6–7, 84,
90–1, 184–5, 193
editing of, 24
fisherman's tale in, 118–24, 126–8
later publications of, 165
mistakes and inconsistencies in,
7, 54, 100, 176, 186
ongoing debate over validity of,
193–4
original documents for, 24–5, 28,
52, 54, 69, 97, 118, 157, 186,
194
printer's mark in, 7–9, *8*
revival of interest in, 186
Zahrtmann's attack on, 184–5,
189–90
see also Zen, Antonio, letters of
Zen palace (near Frari Church),
3, 195
Zen palace (Zen family home), see
Palazzo Zen (Zen family
home)
Zichmni, prince, lord of Sorant,
49–53, 128, 153
in Greenland, 139–41, 150–2
military missions of, 51–3, 63,
69–70, 87–91, 115
theories on possible identity of,
51, 70–2, 78
voyage to North America of,
128–34
see also Sinclair, Henry, earl of
Orkney, lord of Rosslyn
Zurla, Placido, 186

225

ILLUSTRATION CREDITS

Illustration Credits

161 Gerardus Mercator. Private Collection/Ken Welsh/The Bridgeman Art Library.

164 Detail of Mercator's World Map of 1569. Bibliothèque Nationale de Cartes et Plans, Paris, France/The Bridgeman Art Library.

167 Portrait of John Dee (1547–1608) (oil on canvas) by English School (seventeenth century). Ashmolean Museum, University of Oxford, UK/The Bridgeman Art Library Nationality.

181 Vincenzo Coronelli, map of the New World, 1688. Collection of Girolamo Marcello. Photo Pamela Berry.

192 Palazzo Zen. Archive of Sarah Quill. Photo Sarah Quill.

A NOTE ABOUT THE AUTHOR

ANDREA DI ROBILANT was born in Italy and educated at Columbia University, where he specialized in
international affairs. He is the author of two previous
books, *A Venetian Affair* and *Lucia: A Venetian Life in
the Age of Napoleon.* He currently lives in Rome with his
wife and two children.

A NOTE ON THE TYPE

This book was set in Garamond, a typeface originally
designed by the famous Parisian type cutter Claude
Garamond (1480–1561). This version of Garamond was
modeled on a 1592 specimen sheet from the Egenolff-
Berner foundry, which was produced from types thought
to have been brought to Frankfurt by Jacques Sabon
(d.1580).

Composed by North Market Street Graphics,
Lancaster, Pennsylvania
Printed and bound by Berryville Graphics,
Berryville, Virginia
Designed by Virginia Tan

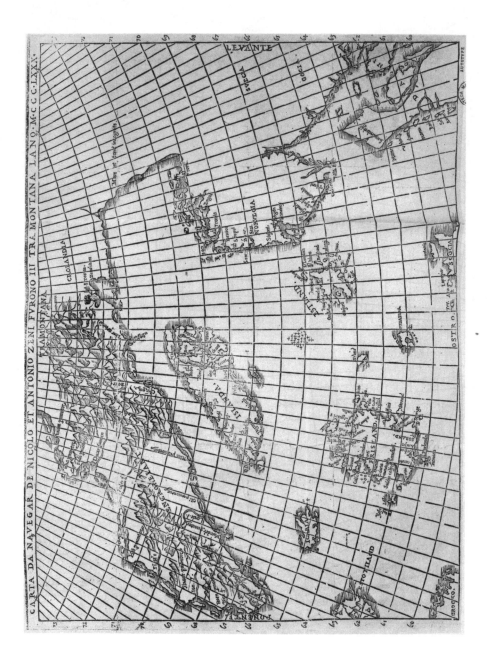

The *Carta de navegar* by Nicolò Zen the Younger,
published by Francesco Marcolini in 1558